THE

CHRISTMAS

CUP

Z A C   M A R K S

"You can overcome anything, if, and only if,

you love something enough."

Lionel Messi

1. NEWS

'You're next, Jed.' Sergeant Brillin is standing at the sidelines with a clipboard, watching us run around the cones and take shots on goal.

'Finally.' I'm desperate to get moving. It's so cold, I can't feel my fingers.

As soon as Dave passes me the ball, I'm away. As I weave between the cones, I can see Miles waiting for the shot. He stands between the posts, a determined look on his face. It might only be training, but he has no intention of letting me score.

It doesn't matter. I'm going to get this in, whether he likes it or not.

I strike the ball hard, aiming for the top right corner. It's not a bad shot, and it's almost on target, only a few feet to the left of where I want it to go. It should go in.

And it would, if it wasn't for Miles.

He springs into the air like he's been taking lessons from Superman, knocking it over the bar.

'Well played,' I say to Miles, giving him a high five as I run past to fetch the ball. He might have robbed me of a goal, but we're on the same team, and he's a friend.

'Good try, Jed,' shouts Sergeant Brillin. 'Another great save, Miles.'

Miles walks towards him. 'Can we call it a day, Coach? I can barely feel my hands, even in these gloves.'

'It is a bit nippy,' admits the sergeant. He's a big, friendly man with a balding head and a decent sense of humour. He's a brilliant coach, and he knows how to keep us all in line. You don't mess with a police officer, even when they're off duty.

'A bit nippy?' teases Luke, Sergeant Brillin's son. 'Easy for you to say, Dad. You could go on an Arctic expedition in that coat!'

Sergeant Brillin shuffles his feet. 'Now, now. I'm not running around, am I?'

'Neither am I,' points out Miles. As he speaks, his breath comes out like a cloud.

'Fair point,' allows the sergeant. 'But you need to get used to these conditions, Miles. It's only going to get colder as winter presses in.'

'Don't remind me.' Miles bangs his gloves together, as if that will help.

'Anyway, that probably is enough training for today. Gather round. I've got some news.'

It doesn't take long for everyone to run over. No-one

wants to hang about.

'What's the news, Coach?' asks Brandon, jumping up and down on the spot to stay warm.

Sergeant Brillin doesn't like to be rushed. He clears his throat. 'As you'll be aware, Christmas is fast approaching.'

'Really? I never guessed.' Brandon gives Sergeant Brillin a mischievous smile, and a few of the boys laugh.

The sergeant raises his eyebrows. 'Any more of that cheek, and I won't tell you the news.'

This time, everyone stays quiet. We want to hear what he has to say. And we also want to get this over with so we can go home. It's way too cold to listen to one of his speeches.

'This year, the Welbeck Council have started a special new tournament for the festive season.'

'The Christmas Cup?' asks Rex. 'I heard something about that.'

'Well, I checked with your parents and I've signed you up for it. I asked them to keep quiet about it as I wanted it to be a surprise. It's a knockout tournament that takes place over four weekends. If you lose any of your games, you're out.'

'Bit harsh,' mutters Ashar.

'But if you win,' continues the sergeant, 'then you play in the final on Christmas Eve. And the winning team get a new kit from the council.'

'Sounds awesome,' says Brandon.

I agree with him. There's nothing I'd rather be doing in the run up to Christmas than playing football, and no team needs a new kit as desperately as us. 'When's the first match, Coach?'

'This weekend. They take place on Sunday afternoons, so they don't conflict with league games.'

Football on Saturday and Sunday. Could my life get any better?

'Are they all local teams?' asks Rex.

'Pretty much. Most of them we've played before. You reckon we can win this thing and get ourselves a new strip?'

'For sure!' says Dave. 'We've got this in the bag.'

'Let's not get too cocky,' warns the sergeant. 'There are some good teams in the tournament.'

'We can still win,' says Rex.

'And we will,' says Dave. 'Foxes forever!'

'FOXES FOREVER!' we shout, echoing him.

We begin to disperse, but Sergeant Brillin calls us back. 'Hold on. There's one more thing we need to sort out before you go.'

Luke groans. 'Seriously, Dad? I can't feel my feet. We just want to go home.'

'You won't want to be doing a Secret Santa, then?'

That gets our attention.

'A Secret Santa?' asks Kris, looking confused.

'I thought it would be fun if everyone got someone else in the team a present, but we did it secretly.'

Kris still looks confused, so Dave does a better job of explaining: 'We all put our names in a hat. Then, everyone pulls out a name. You buy a present for that person and wrap it. That way, everyone gets something, but they won't know who bought it for them.'

'Sounds great,' says Kris, 'but what if you pull out your own name?'

'Then we draw again,' says Sergeant Brillin. 'Are you all up for it? I know pennies are tight, but maybe we set a limit on what to spend. Ten pounds?'

Now, everyone is excited. They all agree enthusiastically, grinning as the sergeant writes out our names on slips of paper.

I wish I could share their excitement, but I can't.
That's because I don't have ten pounds.

I don't even have five.

Christmas is only four weeks away and I have no way to buy my mum a present, let alone another member of the team.

But, what can I do?

The names are already being handed around. I take one

out and unfold it, careful not to let any of the other boys see.

It's the worst one I could have picked: Brandon.

He might be one of my closest mates, but he's also the richest boy I know. He already has everything he wants. Whatever I get him is bound to be a disappointment.

There's a lot of excited chatter as Sergeant Brillin dismisses us.

But, I trudge off the field, thoroughly depressed.

2. SKINT

My house is an embarrassment.

The front yard is overgrown with weeds, but you hardly notice. That's because there are two rusty washing machines right in the middle. We don't have a car and we can't afford to get them collected or taken down the tip.

Paint is peeling from the door, showing yellow underneath the blue.

The only good thing about having a house that looks this rough is that burglars aren't likely to bother breaking in. They know there's nothing of value inside.

I slide my key in the lock and push open the door. Inside, there's no carpet, only floorboards, but I still kick off my boots and pad my way through to the kitchen.

Grabbing one of the glasses from the cupboard, I go to get myself a drink, but discover we're out of squash. Water it is, then.

Mum is out at work, so I have the house to myself, for an hour at least. That gives me time to think. As I stare out the window, I see dark clouds in the distance. It's going to rain soon. At least it didn't happen during practice. There's nothing worse than being cold *and* wet.

But there's another storm approaching: Christmas.

It must be nice to be one of those kids who can look forward to it, knowing they'll get decent presents. It would be great if my biggest worry was whether I got the video game I wanted.

Instead, it just feels like a huge problem, waiting to be solved.

Come on, Jed. Think.

A pile of bills sits on the kitchen table, a reminder of our unpaid debts. We never have money. Everything we get, we already owe to someone else.

Mum tries hard. She works as a cleaner in the village, doing as many shifts as she can. But, without a car, there's a limit to how much she can do.

We don't have spare money for luxuries like Christmas. We barely own any decorations. Last year, we didn't even have a tree.

And presents? We do our best, but they usually suck.

The worst part is, I can't even complain. I don't want Mum to feel guilty, so I have to pretend it's all ok, and that I like whatever cheap gifts I get and that I don't mind having a ready meal for my Christmas dinner.

When I was younger, I didn't notice as much. Now, I realise my friends get ten times more than me, and it hurts.

I don't like to meet up with anyone for a few weeks afterwards, in case they ask me what I got. I'd do anything to avoid that question.

I wander through to the lounge and crash out on the ripped couch. I'm still in my blue and white training kit, but it's not that dirty. I pull a thick blanket over me to stay warm. We don't use the heating unless we *really* have to.

Mum.

That's another thing.

I have to get her a present.

Last year, I remember how guilty I felt when I realised she didn't have anything on Christmas morning. I'd been so wrapped up in my situation that I'd never thought to buy her anything.

That can't happen again.

But that means I have two presents to buy: one for Brandon and one for Mum.

What do you get the kid who has everything?

And what do I get for my mum?

And how can I buy anything when all I have in my money box is seventy-one pence?

I do the only thing a boy can do when faced with questions like these.

I flip on my old console, pick up a controller, and lose myself in a game of FIFA.

***

'Hey, kiddo,' says Mum, as she slams the door. 'Good day?'

I shrug. 'It was ok, I guess. You?'

She walks through to the lounge and gives me a kiss on the forehead. 'It's been a busy one. You staying warm?'

'I'm doing my best. Football practice was freezing.'

'I bet.' Mum wanders into the kitchen and flips on the kettle before coming back through. 'Did Sergeant Brillin tell you about the tournament?'

'The Christmas Cup? Yeah, it sounds great. If we win, we get a new strip.'

'In that case, you better make sure you do.' Mum messes up my hair.

'Hey!' I grin up at her.

'It's not like you'd combed it,' she points out. She settles next to me on the couch and I can smell the bleach on her skin. 'It's weird to think that it's only a month until Christmas.'

I tense up, all the stress returning. I'm not sure what to say, but I know Christmas must be twice as bad for her as it is for me.

'I'm sorry I didn't get you anything last year,' I blurt out.

She gently takes the controller from my hands and puts it on the coffee table before wrapping her arms around me. 'Oh Jed, you don't need to worry about that. I don't want any presents. I'm just happy to be spending Christmas with you.'

I give her a feeble smile, but she's just trying to make me feel better. 'I guess.'

'I know Christmas is hard,' she continues, 'but we'll get by. We always do.'

There's an awkward silence.

'What's for dinner?' I ask, keen to change the subject.

'Pasta bolognese.'

That's good news, at least. 'Sounds great.'

'You know what else would be great?' she says, a twinkle in her eye.

'What?'

'If you took a bath. You're stinking the house out.'

I roll my eyes at her, but I don't protest.

She might be right about me needing to get clean, but she's not right about not wanting a present. She's just saying that so I don't feel guilty.

Deep down, she must long for a gift.

And if there's one thing I'm determined to do this year, it's to get a present for Mum.

3. LIST

The next morning is even colder.

I stuff my fingers deep in my pockets as I shuffle down the street, the tips of my ears already numb.

I'm on my way to the newsagents to ask for a paper round, now I'm thirteen. I had one before, and I did a good job. But I wasn't old enough then, so I had to give it up. I'm hoping that now I'm the right age, I can convince the newsagent to take me back on.

Not that I want to.

Doing a paper round in these temperatures will be brutal. There's nothing worse than getting up stupidly early to bike for miles in the cold and wet. I must be mad.

Still, I need money, and it's not easy to find jobs when you're my age. Especially in a village like ours. If I'm going to buy Mum and Brandon a present, sacrifices need to be made.

The door beeps as I push my way inside. There are lights strung up behind the counter and several shelves are edged with tinsel. There's even a small tree jammed in the corner, covered in baubles.

Albert, the newsagent, is busy serving another customer, so I wait until he's finished, feeling more nervous by the second.

Eventually, he finishes the transaction and turns to me. 'Jed, are you looking for some cheeky snacks for break time?'

I give a feeble smile and fiddle with my tie. 'Not exactly. I don't have any money. That's why I'm here. I wondered if you had any paper rounds going?'

Albert shakes his head. 'Not at the moment. I already have some reliable paper boys. But if a route comes up, I'll let you know.'

'Thanks. You don't know of any other jobs in the village, do you? I'd do anything.' I look at him with desperate eyes.

He frowns, thinking hard. 'Nothing comes to mind, but I'll keep my ear to the ground.'

'Thanks, Albert.'

As I turn to walk out of the shop, he calls my name: 'Jed.'

'What?' I swivel around to see a chocolate bar flying towards me. I snatch it out of the air.

'It's on the house,' smiles Albert. 'Just do me a favour and cheer up, ok?'

I grin back at him. 'Thanks! I'll try.'

Stuffing the bar into my coat pocket, I head back out into the freezing air and shuffle my way to the bus stop.

I don't know how I feel about not getting a paper round. In some ways, it's a relief. I wasn't looking forward to those early starts and long bike rides through the village. But now I'm back to square one: I have no way to earn money before Christmas.

As I wander down the street, I see Brandon, Luke and Dave waiting at the bus stop.

'Alright, Jed?' asks Brandon, who's way too cheery for this early in the morning.

I shrug. 'I guess. You?'

'Yeah, mint.'

'Did you get that maths homework done?' asks Dave. He's worse than my mum, checking up on me. I suppose someone has to.

'Most of it,' I reply. 'I couldn't do those last two questions.'

'They were pretty tough.'

The bus pulls up and we file on, scanning our passes. We make our way to our usual seats. As Brandon slumps into his, I see a flash of neon green just above his shoe.

'Brandon, are you wearing football socks again?' I ask.

He's not embarrassed. He pulls up his trouser leg so I can see. 'Yeah, latest kit. I've got the shirt on under my uniform too. Do you like it?'

'I can't believe you're wearing shin pads to school,' says Dave. 'Are you mad? What do you think is going to happen?'

'We play football at lunch, don't we?' points out Brandon. 'Besides, you know me. I always wear my kit.'

'You better hope Grierson doesn't carry out a sock check,' points out Luke. 'Anything that's not grey or black and you'll get a detention.'

Brandon grins. 'I'll take my chances.'

'Couldn't you have worn them with black grip socks at least?' asks Dave.

Brandon looks insulted. 'I'm not cutting the bottom off these! They're brand new.'

'Just how many kits do you have now?' I ask.

'I haven't counted recently, but over thirty. And I'm hoping to get the new Real Madrid strip for Christmas.'

I see an opportunity to grill him about what else he might want, and I take it. 'What else is on your list for Santa?'

'About a million video games. A new TV for my room. A better phone. The usual stuff.'

'Oh.' My heart sinks. Everything he's mentioned is way out of my price range.

I tune out for the rest of the conversation. I can't help

but feel a pang of jealousy as I think about Brandon's extravagant Christmas list. Meanwhile, I'm struggling to come up with enough money to buy Mum a present.

The bus arrives at school, and we all pile out. I can feel the cold seeping through my jacket, and I shiver as I make my way to the school gates. As much as I hate the idea of spending all day in a classroom, at least it's warm.

The corridors are busy and we have to push our way through to our form room for registration.

'Are you ok, Jed?' asks Dave. 'You were pretty quiet on the bus.'

I decide to tell him the truth. 'I need a job so I can buy some presents for Christmas this year, and I asked at the shop, but they didn't have any paper rounds. Now, I don't know how I'll afford anything for Mum or the Secret Santa.'

Dave looks as if he's going to offer to give me some money, but he stops himself. He knows how I hate charity. 'You'll think of something,' he says.

'I hope so.'

But, truthfully, I don't expect I will.

4. LAPS

The next afternoon, we're running laps.

It's spitting with rain and the cold air burns my throat. I feel myself slowing down, dropping towards the back of the line.

'I can't believe Coach is making us do *five* laps,' pants Theo.

'Tell me about it. He must really want us to be fit for the tournament.'

Theo gives me a sly look. 'Either that or he's mad at Luke and taking it out on all of us.'

'I think he just wants us to get a new kit. We sure need one.'

'True.' Theo slows down to a walk, and I do the same. We can't run any further. 'There are easier ways to get money for a new kit, though.'

'Yeah? Like what?'

'Sponsorship. We could advertise on social media.'

Typical. Theo always thinks the internet solves everything.

'I wish *I* could get sponsorship on social media,' I

mutter darkly.

'Why? What for?'

'Because I need money for Christmas,' I sigh. 'I asked at the newsagents, but there are no paper rounds. And I'm skint.'

'It won't be easy finding a job in this village,' says Theo. 'I do modelling for my dad when I want cash.' He runs his hand through his perfect hair.

That gives me an idea. 'He doesn't need any more models, does he?'

Theo shakes his head. 'I doubt it. I'll ask, but if he needs someone our age, normally he asks me.'

I can guess what Theo's thinking.

'I'm probably not good-looking enough, anyway,' I say.

'It's not that, Jed. Honestly. You'd be fine. It all depends what jobs he has on. Like I say, I'll ask.'

'Thanks.'

Sergeant Brillin barks at us from the sidelines. 'Are you two here to train or to socialise? Get a move on!'

Reluctantly, we start jogging, even though we're miles behind the rest of the team.

A few minutes later, we're gathered around the coach, puffing and panting.

'Our first game is on Sunday,' says the sergeant.

'Remember, if we lose this game, we'll be out of the tournament.'

Brandon interrupts with the question that's on all our minds: 'Who are we playing?'

'The Hessle Sporting Giants. We're going over to their ground for the match.'

Dave and I exchange worried glances. We've been training hard, but the Giants are a tough team. The last time we played them, we got battered. A couple of their players go to my school and I know it won't be easy.

Sergeant Brillin knows that as well. 'Alright, listen up. I know you're all tired, but we need to talk strategy.'

We lean in, doing our best to focus.

'The Giants are known for their strong defence,' he says. 'We need to break through their line. Brandon, Rex, Jed, you boys are going to have to work extra hard.'

I nod, taking in Coach's words. Getting past their defence won't be easy, but we have to try. I lean down and pull up my football socks. There's a small hole in one of them, exposing my cheap shin pads. The sooner we get a new kit, the better.

'We're going to give you boys some practice. You three can try attacking against six defenders and the goalie.'

Rex is shocked. 'Six?'

The sergeant nods. 'If you can get past six players, you'll stand a good chance of getting past the Giants' defence.'

Rex shrugs. 'You're the coach.'

Sergeant Brillin shouts out some instructions, telling me, Rex and Brandon to line up on the halfway line. Then he chooses six of the other guys to take their place in the box. As soon as he blows his whistle, we're off.

It's a hard drill.

With so many defenders, there's no space to move. Every time I run, every time I turn, I collide with one of my teammates who's determined to stop me from getting the ball.

Even Rex is struggling. His fancy footwork and top-shelf skills will only get him so far against the sheer weight of numbers. I watch him move one way, then another, looking for a way past two players. Somehow, he slides the ball through to Brandon.

Brandon is fast. He knows it, and so does everyone else. He can also be greedy. There's no way he's planning to pass, but before he can get in a shot, a defender moves in and boots the ball away.

We go again. This time, Rex gets the ball to me, but I'm sandwiched between Luke and Ashar, and can't move. I try to chip it out to safety, and to sprint after it, but Miles has seen the danger and blocks me with ease.

While a defender fetches the ball, Rex calls me and Brandon over for a quick chat.

'It's not working,' he points out.

Brandon is frustrated. 'How can Coach expect us to take on six defenders and a goalie?'

'He's right, though,' says Rex. 'It's no worse than taking on the Giants.'

'So, what do we do?' I ask. 'We can barely move out there.'

'We play back,' says Rex. 'I'll get the ball almost to the goal-line, then cross it to one of you, at the edge of the box. Make sure you sprint into position at the last moment. Leave your defenders behind. We have to time it just right.'

'Sounds like a plan.'

We line up and let Rex start with the ball again. Then we watch as he weaves his way down the edge of the pitch, darting around defenders. Brandon and I hang back, waiting for our moment.

As soon as I see him glance up, I sprint forwards. I can see Brandon on my right, a blur of blue and white. We've left the defenders behind. I can hear Luke urging his teammates into action.

Rex launches the ball into the air. It's hard and high, but unless we get a move on, we won't be in the box in time. Brandon stretches out his leg, but I get there first, catching the ball on the volley and sending it flying into the top right corner. Miles leaps through the air towards it, but he can't get there in time.

'YES!' It may only be training, but I feel like I've scored in a World Cup final. 'We did it!'

Sergeant Brillin claps from the sidelines. 'That's what I'm talking about. If you play like that on Sunday, we're bound to win.'

I hope he's right.

5. OFFER

At registration on Friday, things get even better. Theo walks over while I'm chatting with Dave.

'I asked my dad about whether he could use you for any of his photoshoots, and he said there might be something coming up that would be perfect for you, if you want to do it?'

'I do,' I say. Then, I wonder if I'm being a bad friend. 'You didn't want the job yourself, did you? I'm not robbing you of some cash?'

Theo shakes his head. 'He says this one wouldn't be suitable for me. He needs someone who looks...' He rubs his ear, not sure how to finish the sentence.

'Poor?' I ask, wondering if I should be offended.

'Younger,' he admits, worried that I'll still take it the wrong way.

I raise my eyebrows and smile. 'Being the smallest kid in the year has its advantages. Who knew?'

'So you're up for it?'

'It pays, right?'

'Yeah, he'll pay. But he needs to chat to you about it

first. He says he wants someone confident for this one. I thought you'd be perfect.'

'Cheers.' It takes a few seconds for what Theo has said to register. 'Wait. Why does he want someone confident?'

'Not much point modelling if you're shy. Sometimes, I've had to model underwear and stuff. It's not for the faint-hearted.'

Now, I'm nervous. There's no way I want someone taking pictures of me in my kecks. 'Will I have to do that? Model underwear?'

'I checked that,' says Theo, 'but he said you'll be in pyjamas for the shoot.'

That presents a different problem. 'I don't have any. I sleep in my boxers.'

Theo slaps me on the shoulder. 'You'll get given those. Don't worry. All you need is a form signed by your mum. Can you head round to mine after school? Dad can give you all the details.'

'Yeah, for sure. I'll come straight there.'

'I'll tell him.'

'Thanks, Theo. You're a mate.'

He grins at me, then heads back to his place.

I should be grateful that he's gone out of his way to help me, and I am. But the more I think about the modelling job, the more nervous I get.

What exactly does it involve? And how much will it pay?

I'm not sure whether to be excited or afraid.

But through all my lessons that morning, I can't think about anything else.

***

After school, I knock on Theo's door.

My stomach feels queasy, and I want to run away, but he's tried to help me out and I have to see this through.

I've never met Mr Becker; Theo's mum always brings her son to games. I wonder if he'll be creepy or strict.

Get a grip, Jed.

Thankfully, it's Theo who opens it. I'm relieved he's here and I won't have to deal with his dad on my own.

'You made it,' he says, sounding surprised.

'I told you I would.'

'Great. Come in.'

'Do I take off my shoes?' I ask, stepping through the door.

'Nah, we're only going to the back garden, anyway.'

'The garden?'

'Dad has his studio out there. You'll see.'

He leads me through the house. I glimpse a massive TV

and leather sofas in the lounge. The kitchen is nice, but it's not as big or impressive as Brandon's. It's still in a different league to my place.

As we step into the garden, I can see a huge log cabin at the far end.

'Dad's studio,' says Theo. He leads the way down the path towards it. 'He does most of his work out here.'

He knocks. 'Dad,' he calls. 'Jed's here. About that modelling job.'

The door flies open. Mr Becker towers over me, a confused look on his face, his messy hair flying in all directions. 'Who?'

'Jed. My mate from football. The small one.' Theo gives me an apologetic smile. 'You said you needed someone for a photoshoot. Something about a new blanket for kids, remember?'

'Ah.' Theo's dad tilts his head and examines me. 'Yes, you'd be just right. You up for some modelling, Jed?'

Mr Becker is nothing like I'd expected. He's wearing a flowery shirt and shorts. He has long hair and weirdly shaped glasses with a slight blue tint. He looks more like a rockstar than a photographer.

'Sure. I'd love to,' I lie.

'Done anything like this before?'

I gulp. 'No. Never.'

'Well, there's nothing to worry about. I've got a client who wants some shots of their new product in action, some new kind of blanket. So, you might need to pretend to be asleep, or just waking up. Sound ok?'

It sounds better than modelling underwear.

'No problem. When did you want to take the photos?'

'This weekend. I need to check with my assistant, when she's available. There have to be two of us, especially when a minor is involved. Are you free on Sunday?'

'As long as it's not the same time as the football match.'

Mr Becker looks confused. 'On Sunday?'

Theo slaps his own forehead with comical frustration. 'It's the Christmas Cup, Dad. I told you all about it, remember?'

'Oh, yes. Of course.'

I get the impression Mr Becker is pretending to recall the conversation even though he has no clue what Theo is talking about.

'How about we text Jed the time you want him once you've arranged it?' suggests Theo. I'm glad he's here to manage everything. Still, there's a flaw in his plan.

'My phone's broke,' I say, a little embarrassed.

'Well, how about I just tell you at the match what time he wants you? The game's in the morning, so it won't be before that.'

'Sounds good,' I agree. 'Do I need to bring anything?'

'Maybe a pair of pyjamas?' suggests Mr Becker. 'If you have anything plain?'

Theo can see the panicked look on my face and he intervenes. 'I told him you'd provide those. Don't worry, Jed. You can borrow mine.'

I smile at him, relieved. 'Thanks.'

Theo turns back to his dad. 'Don't you need his mum to sign a form?'

'Oh, yes, of course. Wait here a second.' Mr Becker heads over to a desk in the corner and rummages around. Now he's no longer in the way, I can see the rest of the studio. It's mostly filled by a large white backdrop which looks like a gigantic piece of paper, much bigger than me, covering one wall and most of the floor. On either side are tripods with expensive looking lights and cameras.

'Now, you're sure you want to do this?' Mr Becker thrusts a crumpled form into my hands. 'You won't let me down at the last minute?'

'If Theo tells me the time, I'll be here, I promise.'

'Good. The client is in a bit of a hurry for this one. They want the social media ads live before Christmas. You would have thought that meant they commissioned it in August, but these executives never think of that. I never understood why they get paid so much.'

'Come on, Jed, let's go,' suggests Theo, sensing his dad is about to launch into a ten-minute rant.

I follow his lead, say a polite goodbye to Mr Becker, and we make our way back up the garden.

'See, that wasn't too bad was it?' he says.

'No, it was fine.'

That's what I say, but I'm still not sure what I've let myself in for.

I guess I'll find out soon enough.

6. CANTEEN

The school canteen is busy. I choose what I want and the dinner lady piles up my plate with sausage, beans and chips. I can't wait to get stuck in.

As I make my way over to where you're meant to pay, someone barges into me, almost making me drop my tray. A couple of chips fall to the floor, but by some miracle I stop the plate falling off.

'Hey!' I turn around to find myself staring up at Tristan, a kid who's always making trouble. He plays for the Welbeck Warriors, our main rivals. They're ruthless on the pitch, always cheating and fouling every chance they get.

'Watch where you're going,' he says, as if it's my fault. 'Wouldn't want you getting injured before the first round of the Christmas Cup.'

'We're not even playing you. Not yet.'

'You think I don't know that? But I've seen the fixture list. If you win your match, and we win ours, then we'll be facing each other soon.'

'I don't care. You'll lose, just like you always do.'

'We'll see.'

I scowl and push past him. He's still behind me when I make it to the till. I put down the tray and pull out the bright yellow card that shows I get free school meals. I might as well hold up a neon sign telling everyone that I'm poor.

'Scrounging food again, Sullivan,' mutters Tristan. 'Do you pay for anything yourself?'

I feel my cheeks burn. Tristan always has the latest stuff: a designer schoolbag, the most expensive football boots, a sharp haircut. It's hard to think of a decent comeback when the guy who's bullying you is one of the most popular kids in the school.

'Some of us don't have a rich daddy,' I say.

He smirks at me. 'From what I hear, you don't even have a dad.'

It's true. My dad left when I was still a baby. But it still hurts. He has no right to make fun of me because I'm from a single-parent family and get free school meals.

I turn around to face him. 'Want to make something of it?'

'What if I do?'

Without thinking, I grab the drink off his tray and fling it in his face. There's a brief moment of satisfaction and I see the look of shock, orange liquid dripping from his hair onto his blazer.

'JED SULLIVAN!'

I swear under my breath. Mr Grierson is storming across the canteen towards me. The entire room has gone silent, and I want the floor to swallow me.

'Sir?'

'What on earth do you think you're doing?'

I shuffle my feet. 'He was asking for it, sir.'

'Was he?' Grierson looks over at Tristan. 'Did he ask you to throw his drink in his face?'

'Not exactly. But he was teasing me about getting free school meals.'

'I have no idea what he's on about,' says Tristan, running his hand through his wet hair, looking every bit the victim.

'Whatever he said doesn't justify this. To my office. Now.'

I look longingly at the tray on the counter. 'But, sir, my food...'

'Leave it here. You should have thought of that before you started a fight.'

I glance sideways at Tristan, hoping I've at least made him think twice about teasing me in the future. But he's not upset. He's smirking, delighted that I've missed lunch and got into so much trouble.

He can't have known I'd react like that.

But I did.

And now, not only will I miss lunch, but I'll probably get a detention as well.

I shuffle away, my stomach rumbling in protest.

***

Grierson does something worse than give me a detention.

After the usual long lecture, he outlines my fate.

'Right, Sullivan. As you're so keen on making a mess in the canteen, you can be on slops duty today.'

'Sir?'

'Scraping plates. Clearing trays. Cleaning tables. Unless you'd rather I called your mum and discussed it with her?'

'No, sir.'

Anything but that.

Mum has enough to deal with, without getting it in the neck from the school as well.

'Well, then, let's get you set up.' He marches me back down the corridor to the canteen. Even the smell of the food makes my mouth water.

He hands me over to a dinner lady who's standing by the recycling point.

'So, the troublemaker returns,' she says, giving me a

disapproving look.

'After the earlier incident, Mr Sullivan here has volunteered to be on clean-up duty this lunchtime,' says Mr Grierson, with relish.

'Well, if he's working here, he'll need one of these.' She rummages around and pulls out a blue stretchy hairnet.

'You can't make me wear that,' I say, starting to panic.

'Why not? All the other staff have them.' She gestures to the counter, and it's true that everyone working there has their hair covered.

'But all the other kids will make fun of me.'

'That's not my problem.' The lady puts her hands on her hips and stares me down. Grierson is glaring at me as well. I pull on the hairnet, wondering if my reputation will ever recover.

I can already hear laughter from across the canteen. 'Let's just get this over with,' I say.

Grierson nods and leaves me with the dinner lady. She shows me how to scrape the leftover food off the plates, and how to separate out the recycling. Before long, students are handing me their trays.

Some of them feel sorry for me; others think it's hilarious that I'm having to do this. I try to ignore them. I don't need sympathy any more than I need mockery. I just never want to feel this embarrassed again.

The worst moment is when Tristan heads over. His tray is overflowing with rubbish. I swear he's made it twice as messy as usual, just so I have more to clear up. His mates are with him.

'Give your rubbish to Jed, boys,' says Tristan. 'He might want to eat some leftovers. He enjoys getting free food.'

They chuckle at his joke, watching me sort through Tristan's trash, my cheeks burning.

'It's not all bad, Jed,' soothes Tristan, sarcasm dripping from his voice. 'That hairnet suits you.'

Now they're laughing like hyenas, and I'm going redder by the second.

'Just get lost, would you,' I hiss. 'You've had your fun.'

'I'd get used to it, if I were you. View it as work experience. If you even know what work is?'

More laughter, and then they're gone.

But I'm still here, wishing I wasn't.

And it feels like lunchtime will never end.

7. GIANTS

Eventually, Sunday arrives.

Today, we play the Giants. And today, I also start my modelling career.

Dave's dad has given me a lift, as always, and the moment I step out of the car, Theo runs over.

'Hey, Jed.'

'Hey.'

'Did you get your mum to fill out the form?'

'Yeah.' I rummage in my boot bag and pull out a crumpled piece of paper. 'Mum was a bit worried about signing it, but I persuaded her in the end.'

'Dad wants you to come straight back to ours after the match. It's the only time he could get an assistant on a Sunday.'

'Oh, right.' I'm not sure how I feel about that. I was hoping I'd get a chance to change and shower first.

'You can come back with us. Mum will give you a lift.'

'Thanks.'

I guess I should be pleased. The sooner I've done my modelling, the sooner I can relax.

'Come on, lads, get a move on,' urges Sergeant Brillin. 'It's almost time for kick-off.'

As I take my place on the field, the air is crisp, but I'm not as cold as I was during training. I've got base layers covering my entire body, as well as an extra sleeveless t-shirt and two pairs of football socks, pulled up as high as they'll go. I wonder if I've overdone it, but if I get too hot, I can always take some stuff off at half-time. I just wish I had some gloves.

I turn to face the opposition. I can see some lads I know from my school: Jacob, the captain. Teddy. Toby. George. Ernie. These are serious footballers and they look sharp in their black-and-white strip.

The ref blows the whistle and we're away.

Dave passes the ball to Brandon, who shoots forwards like a rocket, catching the Giants' defence off-guard. I can see the surprise on their faces as he slips through the gap between their outstretched boots.

Go, Brandon!

He's so fast, though, that he's also on his own. Neither me nor Rex were ready for his sudden burst of energy and we're chasing up the field, trying to give him options.

It turns out, he doesn't need them.

Brandon is at his best, and his worst, when he goes it alone. He dances towards the keeper, his fancy footwork giving nothing away. He dummies a shot, before spinning around and a cheeky back heel secures us our first goal.

1-0 to the Foxes! And we're only a few minutes in!

Brandon turns and gives a dramatic bow. We clap and cheer, but the Giants aren't happy. They have no intention of letting us get away with that.

Jacob shouts instructions to his team and as soon as the ball is back in play, they come at us, fast and furious. They're not planning to make any more stupid mistakes. Not any time soon.

Dave sees the danger and slides in to intercept a pass, but the Giants dodge him and take the ball back. They move it quickly and efficiently, passing it with ease.

I can feel the tension mounting as they approach our goal. The Giants' striker, Toby, takes the ball and shoots, but Miles dives to his left, making a spectacular save.

The parents shout encouragement and clap as Miles jumps up, pumped with adrenaline. He tosses the ball to Dave, who makes his way up the field, dribbling past the Giants' midfielders, before passing it to me.

I hear Brandon calling, but I see a gap in our opponents' defence and I take the chance. I shoot from outside the box, and the ball flies past the keeper's outstretched arms and into the back of the net.

2-0 to the Foxes!

Our supporters go wild, and I turn to Brandon, laughing. 'You're not the only boy who can score,' I shout, and he rolls his eyes.

The Giants regroup and come back at us with fresh determination. They're faster now, more focused than before. They pass the ball back and forth, looking for openings in our defence.

Kris looks worried as he backs up to protect the goal. He's always been our rock in defence, but even he's struggling to keep up with their relentless onslaught.

They see an opportunity and they take it. Jacob passes to Teddy, who shoots towards the corner of the goal. Miles dives, but the ball slips past him and into the net.

2-1.

The Giants' goal is a shock to the system. We can't afford to let them score again, or we'll lose our lead.

We don't get many more chances before the half-time whistle goes.

As we swig our water, Sergeant Brillin gives us one of his pep talks. I don't really listen. We all know what we need to do.

At the start of the second half, our opponents pass the ball around, finding their rhythm. Dave's having none of it. He appears from nowhere, intercepting a pass. A midfielder tackles him hard, but Dave gets the ball back to Ashar.

It's hard work getting the ball to this end of the field. The Giants are relentless, and they press us hard, not giving us any time to think or breathe.

The battle continues for some time until Theo slips past his mark and sends the ball up the line to Rex.

I see Rex signalling me to come forward, and I know what he's after. We need to counter-attack, to catch them off-guard and score another goal. It's time to do what we practiced during Sergeant Brillin's attacking drill.

Rex pushes forwards, making his way into the corner of the pitch. I sprint up the field, dodging and weaving around the defence. It's not easy getting past George and Ernie, but when Rex crosses the ball, I catch it on the volley, bouncing it off the post and into the top of the net.

3-1.

Rex gives me a high five.

Now, we just have to hold on to our lead, and it won't be long until full-time.

To give them credit, the Giants still don't give up. They push on until the bitter end. Jacob even smashes a goal past Miles in the final minute.

But it's not enough to turn the game around.

When the whistle goes, the score is still 3-2 to the Foxes.

It's been hard work, but worth it. We've made it to the second round of the Christmas Cup.

I pump my fist in the air in celebration, grinning at my teammates. When I turn around, I see Jacob standing there, disappointment etched on his face.

'Congratulations, Jed.' He offers me his hand.

I shake it, wishing I had the decency to do that when we lose, but normally I just storm off.

'You played really well,' I say. 'That last goal was epic. You didn't deserve to lose.'

Jacob pulls a face. 'Some days it just doesn't go your way. Good luck in the rest of the tournament.' He walks off to commiserate with his teammates.

As I run my hand through my wet hair, I see Theo beckoning me over and I remember the photoshoot.

I'm sweaty and exhausted and it's the last thing I want to do right now.

But I can hardly back out.

I make my way over, wondering why I ever agreed to do this.

But a promise is a promise.

It's time to see it through.

8. PHOTOS

I'm in Theo's bed.

Thankfully, he's not in here as well, but he is hovering by his bedroom door, watching while his dad takes photos. I thought we'd be doing this in the garden studio, but Mr Becker said it would look better in an actual bedroom.

A female assistant is adjusting tripods, changing the angles of various lights that beam down on me from every direction. I'm not sure why they shut the curtains if they want that much light in here, but I don't say anything. I guess they know what they're doing.

I've changed out of my football kit and into Theo's pyjamas. They're too big for me, but his dad said they look perfect. To be fair, they're not too geeky, more like a baseball uniform than what old people wear. My hair's still a mess, but apparently that's what Mr Becker wants: the *I-just-woke-up* look. Who said that modelling was glamorous?

One thing's for sure. I won't be making the front cover of a style magazine any time soon, not looking like this.

But that's not why I'm here.

Who cares what I look like? It's only for some poxy advert, and I just need the cash.

I'm under the special blanket. It doesn't even have a decent name. Mr Becker called it the P3 blanket, or something like that. I'm no expert, but they really need to rethink their marketing.

'Right, snuggle under the blanket,' says Mr Becker. 'Make it look like you're asleep.'

I do as he asks. I can hear the camera clicking away. Just how many shots does he need?

'Now sit up and stretch for me, Jed,' he says. 'Give a yawn if you can.'

I do my best, but it's hard to yawn on command.

'Now, could you look happy?'

That's almost as difficult. I give a shy smile, finding it hard to relax with so much attention on me.

'Broader smile.'

'Imagine you just won the Christmas Cup,' interjects Theo, trying to help.

That makes me smile.

'Much better,' says Mr Becker, clicking away.

We carry on like that for ages, me following his instructions as best we can as he gets a zillion photos.

There's a pause as he checks the settings on his camera.

'Are we nearly finished?' I ask, curious how long this

will take.

'I've got all the product shots, but now I need some others for the before-and-after reel.'

'Ok, no problem.'

He takes the blanket away from me. 'Right, Theo, could you fetch us a glass of water?'

I'm guessing he's thirsty. Either that, or he's about to offer me a drink. It's been hot under the blanket, and I wouldn't say no.

'Ok, Jed, I'm afraid Melissa is going to need to pour that over your pyjama trousers.'

Wait, what?

'Err, why?' I ask, trying to sound casual.

'So it looks like you've wet yourself.'

It takes a moment for that to sink in. I stall for time. 'I didn't realise that you'd need to do that.'

'Like I say, it's for the before-and-after reel.' Mr Becker says it matter-of-fact, like what he's asking is perfectly reasonable. 'Before you use the blanket, you wet the bed.'

'Oh, right. Is that what the blanket is for?'

Melissa smiles. 'Why else do you think it's called the P3 blanket?'

Then I realise my mistake. They're not saying 'P3'. They're saying 'PeeFree'.

I'm about to be the poster boy for bedwetting.

Literally.

But, this is my first proper paid modelling job and I don't want to mess it up. And it's not like I can walk out halfway through. I try to hide my shock. 'Ok.'

I lean back, and let Melissa pour the glass of water over my crotch. It's the weirdest experience of my life.

Now I know why they chose these sporty pyjamas. The light grey material turns dark in all the right places. Well, all the wrong places if you don't want someone to know you've had an accident.

'Now, sit up and look sad,' says Mr Becker. 'Like you're embarrassed.'

This time, it's easy.

I don't even have to act.

I *am* embarrassed.

If anyone at school sees this, my life is over.

Before she signed the form, Mum warned me that it could be embarrassing to appear in adverts. I told her that it wouldn't matter, because it was just for a blanket. I guess it's too late to do anything about it now.

When the photoshoot is done, I change back into my sweaty football kit and corner Theo in his hallway. 'You can't tell anyone about this. Ever.'

Theo draws his finger across his mouth. 'My lips are sealed. I promise.'

Mr Becker is bringing equipment down the stairs. 'Ah, Jed, heading home?'

I nod. He hasn't paid me yet and I wonder if I should mention it. If I'm going to be publicly humiliated, I deserve some compensation.

Thankfully, Theo comes to the rescue. 'Dad, you haven't given him any cash.'

'Oh, right.' Theo's dad puts down the tripod and rummages around in his pockets. He draws out a £20 note. 'I think that should about cover it.'

I grin up at him. 'Thanks so much.' I can't remember the last time I had this much.

'You did great. Especially for your first time. If you ever fancy doing some more modelling, you just let me know.'

'I will.'

I don't think I will, though. I'm just being polite. The idea of going through all that again makes me shudder.

I say my goodbyes, then head off, clutching the note in my hand.

It might have been a difficult few hours, and I may not have understood what I'd signed up for. But, finally, I can buy some Christmas presents.

And that's all that matters.

9. SHIRT

The next day, I cycle to school.

It's miles away.

Sometimes when people say that, they just mean it's a long way. But our school really *is* miles away, in Welbeck. I've ridden it before, but it always takes longer than I expect.

I could have caught the bus, like normal, but today I want to head into town after school, so I'll need my bike to get home.

Christmas is three weeks away, but I know if I leave it too late to buy a present for Mum and Brandon, all the best stuff will go. Also, I'll be tempted to spend the money on something else.

So, I get up early and bike all the way there, hoping that after school I'll find the perfect gifts.

All day, I keep sliding my hand into my pocket, checking the money is there. I should put it in a zip pocket in my bag, but I don't want to risk anyone stealing it. Besides, I check on it every five seconds. You can't get safer than that.

My method works. When it's hometime, I still have the cash. I cycle out of the school gates and head for the high street. Welbeck isn't a huge town, but it's much bigger than Ferndale. Christmas is a big deal here. Lights are strung between the buildings, making the whole place feel festive.

I chain up my bike near to the huge Christmas tree, then check out some shop windows, hoping for inspiration. There's a place that sells tea and candles, but everything in it is expensive. And I'm not spending the whole twenty quid on a candle. Who does that? Besides, Mum wouldn't want anything like that, and I need to use about half the money on Brandon's gift.

The next shop is a jewellers. I glance at the price tags before moving on. I could model for a year and still not be able to afford any of the items in there.

What, then?

When Theo's dad gave me twenty quid, I felt rich. But now, I'm panicking that I don't have enough to buy one present, let alone two.

There's a hardware store and I consider getting Mum something to help with her cleaning job, but that's hardly an exciting present. I want to get her something she'll love.

It's then that I see it. The charity shop.

I've been in there before, and I know you can get some

great deals in a place like that. But I'm not sure if it's ok to buy second-hand stuff as a present.

Either way, I decide to check it out.

The place has way more tinsel than it needs, every shelf and clothes rail edged with the garish colours. Worse still, cheesy Christmas music is playing over the system. I try to ignore it as I make my way around the shop.

There are racks of women's clothing along one side, but I pass them by. The old woman at the counter is already giving me suspicious looks, and I don't know what size Mum would need.

Then, I see some jewellery in a glass case. Necklaces, mostly. And this time, I can just about afford them. One has a silver chain and a pendant that looks like a diamond, and it only costs twelve pounds.

It's perfect.

I've never bought Mum anything that pretty before, and I know she'll love it. But that will only leave me eight pounds for Brandon's gift. Still, that should be enough.

I head over to the men's clothing, and check out a rail full of sportswear. There's a random football shirt. It's revolting, with neon pink and yellow stripes. I can't tell what team it's from, but it's bright and retro, exactly the sort of thing Brandon wears. There's no way he'd have this already, and it only costs a fiver.

But then I see something else.

No, it can't be.

But, it is. A Manchester City shirt from last season. It looks brand new. Brandon already has one of these, even though he doesn't even support them. But me? I've never owned one as decent as this. I'd give anything for it.

Or would I?

I check the price tag. It costs £7.50. If I get the necklace for Mum, I'd still have enough, but then I'd only have 50p left for Brandon. I won't be able to get him anything for that.

Just do it, Jed.

I'm tempted. Brandon has so much stuff already, it won't really make any difference to him whether he gets anything in the Secret Santa. That kid is spoiled enough as it is. Maybe I could get him a joke present, like a chocolate bar? And, even if he hates what he gets, he won't even know it was me that bought it. It's all anonymous. That's the best bit.

But I can't, can I?

'I'm afraid the shop is about to close, young man.' As if to emphasise the point, the old lady heads over to the door and flips the sign from *Open* to *Closed*.

I'm running out of time and I'm still torn.

I came in here to get presents for Mum and Brandon.

But now, I've seen something I want myself.

'I'd like to buy this,' I say, pointing at the necklace in the glass case.

The woman tuts and sighs as if I've caused her a massive inconvenience as she gets some keys from behind the counter. She eventually finds the one that opens the cabinet and takes out the necklace.

'That will be twelve pounds, please,' she says, holding her hand out for the money before she hands it over.

I can't blame her for being cautious. I pull out the twenty-pound note and give it to her.

She passes me the necklace and sorts out my change.

I'm still wondering which football shirt to buy, but I'm out of time. The woman bustles me out of the shop, before I can ask for anything else.

I'll have to come back another day.

That's probably for the best.

Because I still don't know whether to get the retro shirt for Brandon or the City shirt for me.

And at some point, I'm going to have to choose.

10. TREE

That night, I can't sleep.

All I can think about is the City shirt. I should have bought it when I had the chance. You don't often get opportunities like that.

But, I still don't know what to do about a gift for Brandon. I can't just leave him without a present for the Secret Santa, can I?

I get the bus to school. Even though I'd love to go back into town at the earliest opportunity, on Tuesdays we have football training, so I can't go to the charity shop today. It will have to wait until tomorrow. I just hope the shirt is still available then.

Brandon is especially cheerful this morning.

'Hey lads, guess what I got last night?' he says, a glint in his eye.

'Grounded?' suggests Luke.

Brandon gives him a playful punch on the shoulder. 'Nope. Not this time.'

'A new PS5 game?' says Dave.

'Not yet.'

Dave sighs. 'What then? You might as well tell us. We'll never guess.'

Brandon thrusts out his chest. 'Tickets to the Chelsea game on Saturday.'

'But you don't even support them?'

'I do,' protests Brandon. 'I've been following them all season.'

That's typical. He changes allegiance more often than most people change their underwear.

'So, how come you got tickets?' I ask.

Brandon shrugs. 'Dad got them as a surprise.'

Dave gives him a gentle push. 'You will wear your Chelsea shirt, won't you?' he teases. 'You realise that if you go in any other team's shirt, you'll get beaten to a pulp.'

'I know that,' insists Brandon. 'But I'm hoping I can persuade Dad to buy me a new strip while I'm there.'

'They cost a fortune,' says Luke, incredulous.

'So do the tickets,' I mutter.

I shouldn't be jealous, but I am. Brandon has so much stuff, but he takes it for granted. Now, he's going to watch a match for a team he's only been supporting for a few months. And he'll come out with tons of new stuff as well.

He lives in a different world.

What's the point of buying him anything for Christmas? He already has everything he needs, and more.

As he sits there looking pleased with himself, there's only one thing I want to give him.

That's a punch in the face.

***

Things get even more heated during football practice.

Well, heated may not be the right word, as we're playing in the sleet and I can't feel my hands.

But Brandon is driving me mad.

'Will you just pass the ball?' I shout, as he once again takes a shot on goal. Miles deflects it with ease.

'Chill, Jed. I thought I could score.'

'You always do,' I say, through gritted teeth. 'And then, you always miss.'

That's not true. I shouldn't say that, but I'm mad and it just slips out.

It hits him hard. He struts up to me. 'Yeah? You reckon that you're better than me?'

'I *am* better than you.' I give him a push and he lands on the wet grass.

'Oi, Jed! Pack it in!' Sergeant Brillin is striding over.

'Yeah, what's your problem?' Brandon staggers to his feet, wiping his cold backside.

'*You're* my problem.' I didn't know I was this mad at

him until now. But Brandon has everything I want, and he doesn't even know how lucky he is.

He's one of my best mates, but I hate him.

'Shake hands, both of you,' demands Sergeant Brillin. 'Let's not have any more of this nonsense. If we're going to win the Christmas Cup, we need to work as a team.'

Brandon offers me his hand and reluctantly I take it. Last time two of us had a major fallout, Sergeant Brillin shut us in a room together until we sorted it out. I don't want that to happen again.

'I think we'll call it a day, there,' says the sergeant. 'Give you all chance to cool off.'

I can't get away from the field fast enough. I run off in the opposite direction to usual, before even Dave realises I've gone. I need some time to think, and I want to be alone.

The village church is right next to the field where we play, and I sneak around the side, sheltering from the icy wind by its ancient walls.

I take deep breaths, trying to calm down.

Brandon can be annoying sometimes. Most of the time, in fact. But usually we get on ok. I have no idea why I'm so mad.

Wait.

I do.

It's because I feel like I should buy him a present, even though he's rich.

But that will mean I can't get the shirt I want for myself. And that makes me furious. Especially when he acts so spoiled.

Why does he get everything he wants?

I hear some huffing and puffing around the corner, and I sneak a peek to see what's going on.

Rev Mandy is there, hauling a Christmas tree down the path. She looks like she's about to do herself a serious injury.

I can't just stand here and watch her struggle.

'Do you need some help with that?' I ask, stepping out from my hiding place.

She looks up, surprised. 'Ah, Jed. That would be amazing. Thank you. What are the chances that you would be here at this exact moment? I was praying someone would show up to help!'

'Wouldn't it have been easier to phone someone?'

That makes her giggle. 'You're right, of course. I didn't realise it would be so heavy and then I couldn't work out who to call.'

I grab hold of one end of the Christmas tree, while she takes the other, and together we manoeuvre it through the large wooden doors.

It looks kind of pathetic lying on the stone floor at the back of the church.

'We can leave it here for now,' she says, wiping her forehead. 'I've got some people coming to help put it up and decorate it in the morning. I just needed to get it inside. You're an angel.'

'It's no trouble,' I say. Rev Mandy has helped me out in the past, and it's good to return the favour.

'Have you been at football practice?' she asks.

I glance down at my grubby kit. 'Yeah, we're practicing for a tournament. The Christmas Cup. If we win, we get a new strip for the team.'

Rev Mandy smiles. 'Looks like you need one, if you don't mind me saying.'

'Oh, this is just the training kit,' I explain. 'The match kit is even worse.'

'Well, in that case, let's hope you win!'

'Tell me about it.' We head outside, back into the bitter cold.

'Christmas must be difficult for you,' says Rev Mandy, as she locks up the church.

I look away, embarrassed. She knows that we sometimes use the foodbank. 'It's ok. Mum does her best.'

'She does a great job cleaning the church. But, I don't imagine you get many presents.'

'I don't mind.' It's a lie, but it's a good lie, because that's how I want to feel. Then, I brighten up. 'I earned some cash the other day, so I could at least buy her a present this year.'

'Oh, Jed. That's so thoughtful. You know what Jesus said: it's more blessed to give than to receive.'

'I'm not sure that's always true,' I admit. 'I'm meant to be buying a present for one of my mates as well, but I want to get something for myself instead.' I'm not sure why I feel the need to tell her that, but it feels good to say it out loud.

'That's tricky. But I think you know what your heart is telling you to do.'

'But what if the mate doesn't deserve it?'

'Gifts aren't rewards, Jed. They're gifts. You give them because you love someone.'

'Even if they're being an idiot?'

She bursts out laughing. '*Especially* if they're being an idiot. Anyway, you look like you're freezing to death, standing here in your shorts. I'm getting cold just looking at you.'

'It is chilly,' I say, my knees shaking.

'Thanks again for your help with the tree.'

'Any time.'

I wave goodbye and set off home, breaking into a jog to stay warm.

I guess Rev Mandy is right.
I should follow my heart.
But I don't know if I can.

11. SNOW

The next day, I'm planning to bike in to school, so I can go back to the charity shop.

As soon as I look out of the window, I change my mind. It's torrential rain. I'm not biking in that, not for any kind of football shirt.

The problem is, I have practice again on Thursday, so it will be Friday before I can buy it. That's if it's still there.

It can't be helped.

I jog to the bus stop, my thin coat hardly keeping out the rain. At least I have a blazer underneath, but I'm cold and damp by the time I arrive.

The worst thing about getting the bus is that I have to wait for it. Sometimes that's only for a few minutes, especially if I'm running late. But other times I can be there for ages. There's no way of knowing exactly when it will come.

Standing in the rain is miserable.

It's not just the weather that's getting me down. It's that I know I'll have to face Brandon.

For once, I'm the first one here. Dave's not even around

to keep me in line. But at least I won't have an audience if there's any awkwardness.

I see Brandon coming down the street. He's taking it slow, scuffing his shoes. He glances in my direction, not sure if I'm still mad.

To be fair, I don't know that either. But we both need to get the same bus, and spend every day at school, and play football for the same team. We can't spend all of it fighting.

'I'm not going to hit you,' I say.

'Good to know.' He stands a respectful distance away, just in case.

'I shouldn't have said what I said,' I mumble. It's the closest I can get to giving him an apology.

He shrugs. 'I probably should have passed.'

'So, we're good?' I ask.

'Sure.'

There's an awkward silence.

Dave arrives. He can see that Brandon and I aren't chatting like usual, but he can also see we're not fighting. He does his best to act normal.

'Have you guys seen the forecast for Friday?' he asks. 'They're saying it's going to snow.'

I can't hide my disbelief. 'In December? I doubt it. It never snows before Christmas.'

'That's what they're saying.'

Brandon's face lights up. 'Maybe we'll get the day off school?'

'That would be awesome,' I agree.

It's nice to dream, but we all know it won't happen.

***

It doesn't snow on Friday.

It rains, again. Yet another day when I don't want to cycle into school. The charity shop will have to wait.

But on Saturday, we're playing a league game against a team called Loddon Prime at the Ferndale rec when large snowflakes start to fall.

'I don't believe it,' says Rex.

He's not the only one. It falls thick and fast, and the ref has no choice but to call off the game.

'Sorry, lads. We can't play in this,' he says.

He's right. Our pitch has become a winter wonderland in a matter of minutes. I can't even make out the bright green shirts of the opposition.

To be fair, the ref might have done us a favour. Loddon Prime are a decent team, and their striker, Tommy, has already scored a blinder. If the match hadn't been called off, it would have been hard to beat them.

We run to the sidelines and grab our coats, huddling in

them for warmth as we gather around Sergeant Brillin.

'Not the best start there, boys,' he says, 'but tomorrow we go again. It's our cup match against the Harblebeck Harriers.'

Dave glances around. 'Do you think the snow will have cleared by then?'

'I expect it will melt overnight. If not, I guess we'll rearrange the match.'

When the sergeant dismisses us, I plan to head home. I'm freezing and I just want to get inside. But a snowball smacks me on the back of the head, and I turn to see Dave grinning at me.

'Right, you're dead!' I shout, and bend down to gather some ammunition of my own. Before long, we're all at it. Even Sergeant Brillin joins in the massive snowball fight.

It's fun, but it's not long before my hands are numb and my ears ache with the cold. I can't go on any longer.

'Ok, guys, I surrender,' I say. 'I'm freezing. I need to get inside.'

The words are barely out of my mouth when someone pulls the neck of my coat from behind and shoves a handful of ice down my back.

I cry out and pull away.

Brandon is grinning at me as if he's just told the funniest joke in the world. 'Got ya, Jed,' he says.

'Yeah, congratulations.' I can't help sounding annoyed. 'I already said I surrendered.'

The snow is already turning to water inside my coat. My teeth are chattering as I grab my boot bag and trudge off the field.

I need to get out of here before I say something I'll regret.

And before I kill Brandon.

12. SHOVEL

My house is cold.

I hoped that as soon as I got out of the icy wind, I'd feel a lot warmer. But it's like stepping into a fridge.

'Jed!' Mum runs over as I drop my boot bag and kick off my boots. 'You look frozen! I thought they'd call off the game.'

'They did. But we had a snowball fight.'

I slip off my coat, grimacing as more of the ice slides down my back and into my boxers. Brandon has a lot to answer for.

'You'd better take a hot shower, before you catch your death of cold.'

I'm not going to argue with that. My hands are so numb that it takes a few minutes to pull off my socks and shin pads in the hallway, before I make my way upstairs.

'It's not much warmer in here than it is out there,' I point out. 'Can we turn on the heating? Just for a bit?'

She pulls a face and shakes her head. 'We're already in the red with the energy company. Just put on lots of layers, ok?'

'Sure.'

I know I shouldn't be mad at her, but right now I'd give anything to be in a nice warm house like everyone else. Brandon is probably sipping a hot chocolate with cream and marshmallows in twenty-two degree heat.

I feel a little better as I step under the warm jets of the shower. There's a strange sensation as the water makes contact with my cold skin and numb hands, but my body soon adjusts and I can relax.

For a few moments at least.

'Don't use all the hot water!' shouts Mum. 'We need some to wash up later.'

I allow myself a few minutes more, then force myself to turn off the shower and step out. I dry myself as fast as I can, before my body gets cold.

Dashing to my bedroom, I pull on some base layers, then trackies and a t-shirt, and then a faded hoodie. I tug on football socks to keep my feet warm. Brandon might be on to something with that. I even tuck my trackies into them. Then, I make my way downstairs.

'That's better,' says Mum, as soon as she sees me. 'Want a cup of tea?'

'I'd love one.'

We sit in the kitchen, watching the snow fall outside the window. Even our muddy yard looks beautiful right now.

It's not the nicest house.

And it's way too cold.

But, as I sit next to Mum, sipping my tea, there's nowhere I'd rather be.

***

'Jed! Wake up!' Someone is shaking me. Hard.

Two blurry figures are standing over my bed. I rub my eyes and they come into sharp focus.

Dave and Luke.

In my bedroom.

Something's wrong.

I wonder if I've overslept and the match against Harblebeck is about to start. My phone is broken at the moment and that means I can't set an alarm, but I always wake up way before eleven.

'What's up?' I groan. 'It can't be time for kick-off?'

'It's not. It's just past nine. But we need you, down at the rec.'

'How did you even get in here?'

'Your mum let us in. We couldn't call you because your phone's busted. Now, get up!'

'Why?' I'm warm under my duvet, and I have no desire to move.

'We need everyone. We have to clear the whole pitch.'

'Clear it?' It's taking my brain a while to kick in.

'Of snow.' Dave pulls my duvet aside. As my best mate, he's about the only person who can do that without getting in serious trouble.

'Oi! Do you mind!' I reach for it, but he's pulled it too far away.

Fortunately, I'm wearing my trackies and hoodie; I'm not going to sleep in my boxers in these temperatures.

Dave's not backing down. 'You have to get moving. We all do.'

'I don't understand. Why not just reschedule the match?'

Luke tries to explain. 'Dad found out this morning that it's not possible. There's no time to postpone. That means, if you can't host the game, you lose by default.'

'So, unless we shovel snow right now, we might as well kiss the Christmas Cup goodbye.' Dave puts his hands on his hips and stares down at me.

I almost tell him where he can stick the Christmas Cup, but I know I'm just feeling tired and grumpy. 'Fine. Can I at least pee first?'

'If you're quick.'

'You're a funny boy.' I give Dave a playful shove.

'You should change into your kit, too,' says Luke.

'There might not be time after we've cleared the pitch.'

'This just gets better and better.'

As I take a pee, it's that cold I can see steam rising from it, and I know one thing for sure.

This is no way to start a Sunday morning.

***

When we make it to the pitch, most of the lads are already hard at work.

Sergeant Brillin hands me a snow shovel. 'If you could start near the far goal, that would be great.'

I'm not sure 'great' is the word I would use, but I head over, wondering if there's any chance we'll get the entire pitch clear.

The snow is ankle deep, and we can't just shovel stuff to the side, like you do if you clear a path. The whole pitch needs to be playable, which means the snow needs moving some distance. It doesn't take me long to figure out how hard this is going to be.

I start by shovelling snow like crazy. I figure I just need to work as fast as possible, but I can't keep it up for long. At least my efforts warm me up and I feel able to take off my coat.

Kris glances over. 'It's easier if you push it in lines, like this,' he says. He shows me his method.

'I'll give it a go.'

I push a line of snow from in front of the goalmouth. It's not easy, but it's a little less difficult than trying to throw the snow aside.

'Do you think we'll get it done?' I ask Kris.

'I don't see why not. If we all put in maximum effort.'

I scan the pitch, counting my teammates. 'Someone's missing.'

'That would be Brandon.'

'How come he's not here?' I try not to sound bitter, but I'm already mad at him for not suffering alongside everyone else.

'Dunno. Apparently, he's miles away. But he'll be back for the match.'

Typical.

The boy is going to show up the moment all the hard work is done.

I try to channel my anger into shovelling snow. There's no point getting mad at Brandon again. Not just before a match.

But, somehow, that kid gets all the luck.

13. HERO

'Come on, boys. We're almost there,' calls Sergeant Brillin from across the pitch.

'We?' grumbles Kris. 'I haven't seen him doing much shovelling.'

'He's right, though,' I say, looking around. 'There are only a couple more piles to shift.'

The Harblebeck Harriers are arriving, looking fresh in their purple strip. They stand at the edge of the pitch, watching us work. It's kind of embarrassing, but what can we do? We have to get it finished.

'Coach, we need a rest,' complains Ashar. 'I'm shattered.'

'Well, I can't help that. We'll just have to push through. You can do this. I know you can.'

Dave calls to me. 'Look! It's Brandon!' We see him coming towards us from the car park, a big grin on his face.

'Hey, guys. Sorry I'm late. The traffic was mad.'

'Where have you been?' I demand. I want answers. And I want them now.

'In a hotel. I went to see the Chelsea match, remember?'

'Wasn't it called off?' I ask.

'Nah, snow's not as bad there, else we wouldn't have gone. As soon as you go past Welbeck, everywhere is clear. What's going on here?'

'We've had to clear the whole pitch,' explains Dave. 'If not, we'd have had to forfeit the match and get knocked out of the tournament.'

'Awesome job.' Brandon's trying to be positive and encouraging, but I still want to kill him.

'Was the hotel nice?' I ask. 'Were the beds comfy? Did you get a good night's sleep?'

Brandon is oblivious to my sarcasm. 'It was amazing. Four-star. There was a luxury spa and everything. And the cooked breakfast was the best I've ever had.' The boy strips off his trackies and pulls on his boots. 'And I got Dad to buy me the new Chelsea away strip. It's epic. Are you alright, Jed? You look cold.'

'That's because I've been shovelling snow.' I almost growl the words.

'Looks like you got the whole pitch clear,' he says.

He's right about that. There's hardly any snow left, but I can see Sergeant Brillin chatting to the ref, his forehead creased with concern. Something is still wrong. A few seconds later, he calls us over.

'Ten out of ten for effort,' he says. 'You did a great job

clearing the pitch. But I've got some bad news, I'm afraid. The ground is still frozen. Much too dangerous to play on, apparently.'

We all groan in frustration.

'Does that mean we forfeit the match?' asks Dave.

The sergeant nods. 'I'm afraid so.'

More groans. I curse under my breath. All that effort for nothing!

'Wait a sec,' says Brandon. 'It didn't snow everywhere. When we drove back from London, the snow only started in Welbeck. Couldn't we use a different pitch?'

Sergeant Brillin looks thoughtful. 'It's a bit last minute, but you might be on to something. I get on well with the coach from the Brookland Beavers. I wonder if their pitch is available.' He pulls out his phone and turns away.

We wait, listening in.

There are a few frustrating minutes while he exchanges pleasantries, but then we hear him getting down to business, explaining our urgent need for a pitch. When the sergeant hangs up the phone, he's smiling.

'Great news, lads! The Beavers' pitch is available, and they didn't have any snow yesterday. They played on it this morning.'

We cheer, while Sergeant Brillin hurries over to the referee to explain the change of plan.

Fortunately, both the referee and the Harblebeck Harriers want the game to go ahead, so they're happy to agree to the change of venue. I thought they might say no, so that we had to forfeit the match, but I guess they want to win the Christmas Cup fair and square, not due to a freak occurence of the weather.

As we climb into Dave's car, Miles slaps Brandon on the back.

'Great thinking, Brandon,' he says. 'I think your idea just kept us in the competition!'

'Meh,' says Brandon, with a cheeky smile. 'It's not easy being a genius.'

I snort and look away.

Dave gives me a warning look. Brandon might not have picked up on my reaction, but nothing gets past Dave.

He hisses in my ear. 'I know you're annoyed with Brandon, but don't mess this up.'

'I'll do my best.'

And I will.

But my emotions aren't that easy to control.

***

It's dry and sunny when we reach the village of Brookland. It's hard to believe it's only a ten-minute drive from

Ferndale, but there's no sign of snow.

The Beavers pitch is a little damp, but it's soft and the ref has no hesitation in allowing the game to go ahead.

Harblebeck kick off, and they're not messing about. Quick, clean passes and carefully planned manoeuvres leave our midfield running around like headless chickens.

They pass it forwards, determined to score in the first few minutes of the match.

Fortunately, our defenders are having none of that. Miles shouts out orders from the goal and our defenders do as they're told. All the Harblebeck strikers are marked when the cross comes through, and Luke boots it away.

Harblebeck get a throw in, but it's so far up the field, it hardly matters.

Still, we all know what the match will be like.

We're going to be chasing our tails, fighting off attacks, struggling to keep our heads above water.

The problem is, we're tired. We've not come into this game fresh, like Harblebeck. We're been shovelling snow for hours and our bodies are already aching.

Normally, I'd play football until I drop, but if I could choose right now, I'd go home and drink cocoa. Sadly, that's not an option. We just need to press on and make the best of it.

Somehow, Theo gets the ball to Rex. I force my legs into

action, running alongside to give him support. Brandon is even faster. He bounds up the field like an energetic puppy, calling for the ball.

It's clear who's in the best position to score, and it's no surprise when Rex passes to him instead of me.

It's also obvious that Brandon has more energy than the rest of us put together. He cuts through the Harblebeck defence like a Tasmanian devil, darting and spinning past outstretched legs and late tackles.

I glance at the Harblebeck keeper and see fear in his eyes. He can tell Brandon is a genuine threat. But he's not sure whether to move forward or back. He doesn't know whether to trust his defence.

That moment of hesitation costs him dear. Brandon catches him out, dummying a shot and then flicking it the other way.

As the ball lands in the net, we can't believe our luck. Somehow, we've scored the first goal.

Rex grabs hold of Brandon and ruffles his hair in celebration. I jog over and give him a fist bump, the most enthusiasm I can muster.

I know I should be happy that Brandon just scored, and it's a good thing that at least one of our players isn't exhausted from the start. But, I'm still mad he missed all the hard work, and now he's returned like the conquering hero.

The Foxes have never been one of those teams that only have one decent player. You know the type: their strategy is to just get the ball to the same kid, over and over. That's not us, and that's not how we play.

But, today, it's the only thing we can do. With so many of us feeling knackered, it's clear that only Brandon can save us. And he's loving it.

Harblebeck haven't given up, and they score a couple of goals themselves, carving up our lacklustre defence. Miles is working harder than anyone else on the pitch, saving more shots than any goalie should. But he can't get them all.

With five minutes to go until full-time, the score is 3-3, and none of us can face the prospect of extra time.

'We have to get one more,' shouts Dave. 'And fast.'

I nod at him. We're determined. But so are our opponents. Whoever loses this match gets knocked out of the Christmas Cup.

Rex nudges me. 'If you get the ball, pass it to Brandon.'

I resent that. I can score as many goals as he can. But I know why Rex is saying it. Neither of us have as much energy as he does. We're spent. And Brandon's on fire.

Our midfielders work some magic. Despite the Harriers' determination, Theo blocks a pass, and Dave picks up the loose ball, booting it up the field to me.

I use the last of my energy to sprint forwards. I can see Brandon hurtling towards the box, but I could score this myself, and take all the glory.

'Pass to Brandon!' I hear Rex shouting.

I only have seconds to decide.

The goalie stares me down, daring me to shoot.

I imagine what it would be like to put the ball past him, cannoning it into the top right corner and hearing the cheers of my teammates.

But, no.

Not today.

With the last of my energy, I slide the ball to the left. It's not perfect, but it's enough. Brandon takes control like a pro. He only needs two touches to send the ball where it needs to go, into the bottom left corner.

The boys go wild.

4-3.

The last three minutes of the game are tense. We don't want to give away our lead. Harblebeck push our defence to their limit. They manage one last shot on goal. Somehow, Miles snatches it from the air.

When the final whistle blows, I collapse on the cold ground, exhausted. I'm too tired to celebrate, too tired to speak.

A few of our guys congratulate Brandon. He scored all four goals, so it's no surprise he's the man of the match.

I groan, despite our win.

That lad has done it again.

And we'll never hear the last of it.

14. BET

By Monday, the snow has melted.

That's good, because it means I can bike into school. I'm desperate to get back to the charity shop to see whether they still have the shirt.

It also means I don't have to sit near Brandon on the bus and listen to him bragging about all the goals he scored.

I'm wearing my goalie gloves as I cycle in. They're not designed for warmth but they're the only gloves I have, and they're better than nothing. I got given these when I had to play in goal when Miles was grounded.

In fact, it was Brandon that gave them to me.

And he gave me some base layers, and loads of other kit.

Whatever else you say about Brandon, he's generous.

But, does it count when you have so much stuff?

You have to buy him a present.

My conscience isn't going to let up. I can't leave my mate empty-handed at the team's Secret Santa. But if I buy him something, I won't be able to afford the Man City shirt. And I've never wanted anything as badly as I want that.

Why should I spend all my money on him? He already has so much stuff already. It's not fair.

I keep changing my mind, not sure what to do.

***

When hometime comes, I'm still undecided.

This time, as I wander down the high street, I don't look in any other windows. There's no point. I can't afford anything those places sell.

When I get to the charity shop, I head straight over to the sportswear rack in the corner. I'd been hoping that they might have sold the City shirt. That way, I wouldn't be tempted to buy it. But it's still there, just as pristine as I remember. There's a full-length mirror nearby, and I can't resist pulling the shirt off the rack and holding it up in front of me. I double-check the price tag. It would be awesome if all the shirts were half price, so I could buy both this and the one for Brandon.

But, sadly not. This shirt would still cost me almost all the money I have left. And I can't get anything for Brandon with 50p.

Reluctantly, I check out the rest of the rail.

I already know it's there. I can see the pink and yellow stripes a mile off. But, I always knew it would be. Who else would be mad enough to buy anything like that?

I hate it, but Brandon will love it, and that's what matters.

I look at both shirts, weighing up my options. I can't buy them both, that's for sure.

If I don't buy the Man City shirt, I may never get the opportunity to own a shirt like this again. But, if I do, then I'll have no cash left for the Secret Santa.

I think you know what your heart is telling you to do.

Rev Mandy's words pop into my head, just when I don't want to hear them.

Cursing under my breath, I hang the Manchester City shirt back on the rail and take the horrific pink and yellow thing over to the counter. The old lady at the till gives me a strange look, as if she's as confused about why anyone would want this as I am. But she hasn't met Brandon.

I can't pay her fast enough.

If I don't, I might change my mind.

I stuff the shirt into my school bag, and as I walk out of the shop, I don't even glance over my shoulder. I can't bear to even catch a glimpse of the City shirt, knowing that I'll never see it again.

***

As soon as I step outside, I hit trouble.

Tristan and his cronies are coming down the street. He glances up at just the wrong moment. He's seen me, and he's not going to miss out on another opportunity to humiliate me in front of his mates. 'Look who it is. Jed Sullivan.'

They walk over to me, and I freeze.

'Been shopping?' asks Tristan.

'None of your business,' I mutter. 'Just leave me alone.'

'Maybe he's bought a new hair net?' says Bryant, one of Tristan's mates. That gets a laugh, and I feel myself turning red.

'The charity shop,' observes Tristan. 'Bit expensive for you, isn't it? Don't you normally get stuff for free?'

'No.'

'Yeah, you do. I saw you at the foodbank, remember?'

He did. Just one time. And he's never let me live it down. I try to push past, but he blocks my way.

'Listen up, Sullivan. We're playing your pathetic excuse of a team this Sunday. And you're going to lose. Badly.'

I glare at him. 'Want a bet?'

Tristan smirks. 'I would. But I know you don't have any money, so you wouldn't pay up.'

More laughter.

I can't take it any more. I want him to be embarrassed for a change. 'How about if we win, you kiss my boots? Right there, on the pitch, in front of everyone. But if you win, I'll kiss yours.'

The words are out of my mouth before I can stop them.

Tristan frowns, considering the offer. 'How do I know you'll do it, and you won't back out?'

I shrug. 'I could ask the same. But all your mates are here. They're witnesses.'

He hesitates, but his mates are egging him on.

'Come on, Tristan. We'll bury them,' says one.

'They don't stand a chance,' adds another.

Still, he's unsure.

'Scared?' I ask.

That does it. Tristan holds out his hand. 'Fine. Loser kisses the winner's boots.'

I shake his hand. 'Deal.'

'You shouldn't have agreed to that, Jed,' he taunts, as I walk away. 'You'll regret it on Sunday.'

I don't respond.

But I know he's right, because I already regret it.

Playing the Welbeck Warriors will be difficult enough as it is, without the added pressure of public humiliation if we lose.

I could kick myself for being so stupid, but I'm fed up

of being teased by him and his mates, and I wanted to see him squirm for a change.

I unlock my bike and start the long cycle ride back to Ferndale, more determined than ever that the Foxes have to win.

15. HUMILIATION

'Have you got plans for Christmas day?'

The question catches me off-guard. It's Sunday, and Dave's dad is driving me to the match.

I shuffle in my seat. 'Not anything special. Me and Mum will spend it at home.'

'No other family visiting?' asks Mr Hughes, surprised.

'We don't have any,' I say. 'Not after my nan died a couple of years back.'

'Maybe you and your mum could join us?' suggests Mr Hughes. 'The more the merrier.'

It's a kind offer, and there's nowhere I'd rather be at Christmas, but I can't help wondering if he's only offering because he feels sorry for me. I'm not a charity case and I don't want to intrude on their family time. 'Err, maybe. I'm not sure.'

'Well, ask your mum,' says Dave's dad, cheerily. 'It would be great to have you, Jed. Really.'

'Yeah, it would be awesome,' adds Dave. 'See if you can persuade her.'

We get out the car and head over to where the other

boys are waiting. I feel more nervous than ever. We're at the Welbeck ground, and there are loads of parents watching.

'It's the semi-finals, lads,' says Sergeant Brillin. 'If you beat Welbeck, we're through to the final on Christmas Eve!'

That's one reason to win.

But there's something just as important. I can see Tristan warming up with his teammates. If I lose, I'm going to have to kiss his boots. I never want to do that.

'How are you feeling?' Dave puts his hand on my shoulder. He knows about the bet. He probably thought I'd been stupid to agree to it, but he also knew there was no point saying that. Instead, he tries to be a friend.

'Not great.' I reach down and tug my orange socks higher, over my knees.

'At least this week we haven't been shovelling snow,' he points out.

He's right. We'll be playing fresh this week, and that should make all the difference. We've beaten Welbeck before, so we know it can be done.

But, it's never easy. They're brutal.

We know there's a high probability a few of us are going to get badly injured. That's how Tristan's team play. It's all rough tackles and sneaky fouls, anything to win.

'You haven't forgotten our deal, have you, Sullivan,' says Tristan, as we take our places on the field.

I try to act confident. 'Nope. I'm looking forward to seeing you kiss my boots.'

'That's not gonna happen. You'll be kissing mine. But you know the funny thing?'

'What?' I ask, stupidly.

'That still won't be the most embarrassing thing that's happened to you this week.'

I stand up for myself. 'If you're on about the charity shop, you can shut your face. There's nothing wrong with buying stuff there.'

'I'm not talking about that.'

What, then?

The ref is about to blow the whistle.

Tristan gets in one last remark. 'Still wetting the bed, Sullivan? Why doesn't that surprise me?'

I freeze.

He's seen the photos that Theo's dad took.

But how? Theo would never sell me out.

'Jed!' Dave's frantic shout brings me back to my senses. The game has started, and he's passed me the ball, but I've been distracted by Tristan, and I fail to make contact. It sails past me for a throw in.

'Sorry,' I say, my head spinning.

Dave looks disappointed. 'Come on, mate. Get your head in the game. We need to win this.'

But I can't concentrate. While one of the Welbeck players fetches the ball, I turn back to Tristan.

'I don't know what you're talking about.'

He raises his eyebrows. 'You've not seen the latest PeeFree adverts then?'

No. This can't be happening.

'How do you know about that?' I demand. I stand in front of him as his teammate prepares for the throw.

'Everyone knows, Jed. It's all over the school. One of the lads saw it and shared it online. You look really sweet in your *wet* pyjamas.'

As the Welbeck player throws the ball towards us, Tristan knees me in the back as he jumps, knocking me to the ground. The ref doesn't call a foul, leaving him free to turn and sprint up the field.

While our defenders move in to tackle him, Dave turns to me. 'Are you ok? You look like you've seen a ghost.'

'It's Tristan. He says there's something going around the school about me wetting the bed.'

Dave says nothing. That's not a good sign.

I glare at him. 'You knew?'

Ashar has cleared the ball, and it sails through the air in our direction. Dave dashes off to rescue it before he can answer my question.

Even though I'm free, he passes it to Rex.

Then, he comes closer. 'Yes, I knew. We all did. But if we told you, it would hardly help you focus, would it?'

I huff and turn away.

I know he's just trying to be a good mate, but I'd have rather found out what was going on from him than from my worst enemy.

Rex still has the ball, but he can't get close to the goal. Both me and Brandon try to move into space, but I can feel someone breathing down my neck.

It's Tristan.

'Try not to wet yourself,' he hisses in my ear.

That puts me off. As Rex crosses, I mis-kick it. It's the worst shot ever, closer to the corner flag than the goal.

Tristan smirks. He knows he's getting to me. 'How do you stop it happening when you're playing football?' he asks.

I think he's talking about my terrible shot, and I'm confused. 'Stop what happening?'

'How do you make sure you don't wet yourself? Do you wear nappies?'

My chest feels tight. Blood rushes to my head. 'Just get lost, Tristan. It's not funny.'

'Everyone else thinks it is.'

That's the problem. It's bad enough knowing that Tristan and his buddies are making fun of me. The idea that everyone else in the school knows is more than I can bear. If they've shared the advert over the weekend, what will it be like on Monday morning?

Why did I ever agree to do it?

I know it's my fault. But, I wasn't expecting anyone at school to see the photos. Why would they? The internet is a weird thing. Once something is out on social media, you never know when it's going to come back to haunt you.

I should have known that.

I did know that.

But I did it anyway.

I'm still thinking about how terrible my life is when Theo sends the ball in my direction. I spin and weave past a couple of Welbeck players, jumping just in time to avoid being crippled by one of their defenders.

'Go, Jed!' shouts Dave, spurring me on.

'Someone tackle nappy boy!' says Tristan. 'Quick, before he has an accident.'

Nappy boy?

He can't call me that. If people start calling me that, my life is over.

I'm so distracted, I fumble the ball. Instead of blasting it into the back of the net, I send it rolling towards the goalkeeper. It moves so slowly, the defenders laugh.

I turn on Tristan, my whole body shaking.

'DON'T YOU DARE SAY THAT AGAIN!'

Tristan gives a wicked grin. 'Feeling sensitive? I think someone needs his nappy changed.'

I'm about to launch myself at him. I can't take it anymore. He needs to pay. But Dave and Brandon are holding me by the arms, pulling me back.

'Calm down, Jed,' says Dave. 'If you hit him, you'll get a red card. That's what he wants.'

I glance back. The smug look on Tristan's face almost sends me over the edge. My eyes sting with tears of frustration.

Dave's right. Tristan is winding me up, so I'll do something stupid and get sent off.

I have to cope with the name-calling and the snide remarks. I can't let them get to me.

But they do.

I may not hit Tristan, but neither can I focus. Every time I get the ball, I mess up. The Welbeck players are smirking at me the whole time.

After a while, my team stop passing as well.

They know it's the only way we'll win.

It turns out they're right.

Between them, Rex and Brandon score two. And

Welbeck only get one past Miles.

As the game draws to a close, their tackles get wilder and their attempts more desperate. They push and trip, slide and pull, all out of sight of the referee.

But it doesn't do them any good.

We win 2-1, no thanks to me.

But, when the ref blows his whistle, I suddenly remember what that means.

'Hey, Tristan,' I shout. 'Looks like we won.'

Tristan grimaces. 'It wasn't a serious bet.'

'Let's ask your mates, shall we?' I can see them watching. His buddies may not like me, but they're not going to respect him either if he doesn't go through with this, and he knows it.

The tables have turned.

I may be the bedwetting kid, but he's about to be the boot-kissing bully.

'Fine. I'll do it.'

I hold my leg forward. He looks down at it, then drops to the floor and kisses my boot so fast it's hard to believe it's happening. A second later, he's back on his feet.

He's hoping no-one will notice, but the Foxes cheer and even his mates are smirking behind his back.

Tristan does not look happy. 'You think you've won, Sullivan, but you're going to pay for this.'

He storms off. It's the best thing that's happened all day.

'You did well to hold it together,' says Dave, slapping me on the back.

'Not exactly. I was rubbish. Couldn't concentrate at all. Not with everything else.'

'Hey, we won. That's all that matters.'

That's easy for him to say.

It's not his reputation that's in tatters.

But at least *something* has gone right.

16. SHOCK

Monday is horrible.

As soon as I get on the bus, I can sense everyone's eyes on me. They've all seen the video.

It's going to be like this all day. All week, even. Maybe longer.

After the match yesterday, Dave showed me the advert. It was bad. A video of me, sitting up with a wet patch. The voiceover. 'Does your child still wet the bed? Try out the new PeeFree Blanket, a dry night guaranteed.' The video cuts to me waking up under the blanket. This time I'm happy and my pyjamas are dry.

I almost died with embarrassment. Millions of people have seen this by now. I'm famous for all the wrong reasons.

'How you feeling?' asks Dave, as I drop onto the seat next to him.

'Like an idiot. Everyone's going to be laughing at me behind my back.'

'What did Theo say?' asks Luke.

'He was really apologetic. He was only trying to help me

out, to be fair. He didn't know it would be such an embarrassing advert. Even his dad didn't realise this would be such a high-profile campaign. They didn't think anyone I knew would see it.'

'I hope he paid you well,' said Brandon.

'Twenty quid,' I reply.

'Is that all?' says Brandon. 'I wouldn't wash up for that kind of money.'

'You get paid to wash up?' I look at him, incredulous.

'Sometimes.'

That boy is so rich, they probably use bank notes as toilet paper. I'm already regretting having spent the money on his present.

I groan as I think about the day ahead. 'My life is over.'

'It's not that bad,' Dave reassures me. 'After a few days, everyone will forget about it and move on. Trust me.'

'I don't think Tristan will,' I point out.

'He sounded pretty mad he had to kiss your boots. He kept on about getting revenge.'

I snort. 'He'll call me nappy boy for the rest of my life.'

'Just ignore him. He'll stop eventually.'

It's good advice, and I plan to follow it. Tristan's always called me names, ever since I started at that school. He always mocks me. As long as it's just him, I can live with that.

Sure, I'm going to get some extra attention this week, while the advert is fresh in people's minds. But, with any luck, by the weekend, everyone will be bored with it.

And I'll never need to be that embarrassed again.

Dave changes the subject. 'Did you ask your mum about coming to ours for Christmas?'

'Yeah. She's well up for it, if you're sure we're not intruding?'

'No, mate. I need someone else my age around.'

'It's a deal then.'

'I'll tell my parents.'

I don't want to make a big deal out of it, but Dave's family have rescued my Christmas.

I finally have something to look forward to, and he has no idea how grateful I am.

***

At football practice on Tuesday, we get a shock.

Sergeant Brillin gathers us around and pulls a tatty piece of paper out of his tracksuit pocket. 'Right, lads, I've had a letter from the council and there's a bit of an unexpected development with the Christmas Cup.'

'What do you mean, Coach?' asks Brandon. 'We're still in the final, aren't we?'

'Yes, yes. Don't worry about that. We're due to play Falford Town on Christmas Eve. I've sent all your parents the details.'

'So, what's the problem?' asks Theo.

'Hmm. Well, you're not going to like this.' Sergeant Brillin looks nervous, like he doesn't know how to break the bad news.

Luke says what we're all thinking. 'Just spit it out, Dad. Please.'

Sergeant Brillin nods. 'Ok, then. The cup final is a bit of a publicity stunt for them, supporting youth sport and raising money for charity and stuff.'

I feel like I'm going to explode. We already know all that.

'And?' prompts Dave, trying to hurry the sergeant.

'And, well, there's no easy way to say this, but they think it would be fun if everyone looked a bit Christmassy.'

I relax. 'That's ok. We can wear some tinsel or something.'

He shakes his head. 'No, Jed. They're after something a bit more, err, full-on.'

'Like what?' demands Ashar.

Sergeant Brillin looks around at us. 'They want you to dress up as elves.'

Silence.

No-one speaks for several seconds. It feels like an age.

'You can't be serious,' says Rex. He almost whispers it.

Luke is horrified. 'Do we have to?'

'Rules of the competition, apparently. The Christmas Cup final. Santas versus the elves. Hidden somewhere in the small print.'

'But how can we?' I blurt out. 'I doubt any of us have elf costumes at home.'

And I can't afford to buy one.

That's what I'm thinking, but I don't say that last bit. I don't need to. Everyone already knows.

'I can get the costumes,' says Brandon. 'I think you can buy them online pretty cheaply. I'll ask my parents. They won't mind.'

'That's a kind offer, Brandon,' says the sergeant, looking relieved. 'But there's no point unless these boys are up for wearing them.'

'I'm not dressing as an elf,' says Ashar.

'Me neither,' agrees Kris. 'It's way too embarrassing.'

'If you don't, we lose the competition,' says Sergeant Brillin, sadly. 'We won't get a new strip.'

'Come on, lads,' says Dave. 'We can do this. It's not like any of us will be on our own. We'll do it as a team.'

'Yeah,' agrees Brandon. 'It'll be a laugh.'

'I dunno,' says Harry. 'We'll never live it down.'

'Harry, mate, you have to do it,' insists Brandon, with a mischievous grin. 'It can't be worse than wearing a Spurs shirt.'

That makes everyone laugh, even Harry, who throws his water bottle at Brandon.

'I think we need to have a vote,' says the sergeant. 'Who's up for playing as elves?'

Brandon and Dave put up their hands. Most of the other boys follow suit.

I don't want to do this. I hate dressing up. Whenever we had World Book Day at my primary school, I'd always go in football kit. But, if the rest of the team are up for this, I'm not going to let them down. Reluctantly, I raise my arm.

Even Ashar, Kris and Harry put their hands up in the end.

'That's settled then,' says Sergeant Brillin. 'Thanks so much for being such good sports. I'll have a word with Brandon's parents, and see whether they can help us with the costumes. We'll be training again on Thursday, but that's the last practice before the game next week.'

'This better be worth it,' mutters Ashar.

'Tell me about it,' says Kris.

As we grab our stuff and head home, I can't help wondering how I keep ending up in such embarrassing situations.

Just when I thought the worst was over, the universe drops me in it again.

It seems there's nothing I can do but accept my fate.

17. ELVES

We all have second thoughts about our decision the moment we see the costumes. We're at Luke's house, where we arranged to meet before the match, when Brandon arrives with a large box.

'You can't be serious,' says Kris, as he pulls out the green top and red-and-white striped tights. There's even a hat with a bell on it.

'It was the best we could find,' says Brandon, a little defensive.

'I'm not wearing that,' says Kris. 'I have too much self-respect.'

'It's just for a laugh,' says Dave. 'The other team will be dressed up as well.'

'Besides,' adds Luke, 'we have to wear them, in order to win the Christmas Cup, remember?'

Ashar crosses his arms. 'Yeah? Well, put it on then.'

'Fine, I will.' Luke snatches one of the costumes. Right there in his living room, he gets changed. Luke isn't shy, and he strips down to his boxers before pulling on the tights and the green top that almost hangs down to his knees.

We don't tease him. We're impressed he's had the guts to do it, and in a few minutes we're all going to look like that.

'What about shin pads?' asks Harry, a little uncertain.

'I guess they could go under the tights,' says Luke. 'I'll try it.'

While he's doing that, the rest of us get changed. Even Kris gives in, but he doesn't look happy.

By the time Sergeant Brillin re-enters the room, he's greeted by a team of Santa's little helpers.

'You look amazing!' he chuckles.

'Not what I'd call it,' mutters Ashar.

'I know you didn't all want to do this,' says the sergeant, 'but I have massive respect for all of you. When Brandon showed me the costumes, I thought you'd bail, if I'm honest.'

'We almost did,' admits Kris.

'I still can't believe you bought ones with tights,' says Harry, giving Brandon a dark look.

Brandon shrugs. 'Hey, you try finding an elf costume without them.'

'Anyway, we should all be grateful to him for getting hold of these at such short notice,' points out Sergeant Brillin.

A few of the boys voice their thanks and slap Brandon on the back. Kris and Ashar look like they'd rather kill him than thank him. I know how they feel. The tights are itchy and we look ridiculous.

The idea of playing a football match like this is insane.

'Right, come on boys. We need to get moving,' says the Sergeant. 'Lets not keep your parents waiting outside.'

***

We arrive at the Welbeck ground fifteen minutes before kick-off.

It's a sunny Christmas Eve and as we pile out of the cars, I already feel self-conscious in the elf costume. I guess I better get used to it. We have to play the whole match like this.

To make it worse, there are way more spectators than before. Because it's the final, the council have made it a community event with food vans and stalls set up at the edge of the pitch. The place is heaving. Christmas lights sparkle and a brass band plays carols at the far end.

People smile and point as we head over. I guess they've never seen so many elves before, and they wonder why we're dressed up.

'I feel like an idiot,' mutters Miles.

'Well, you look like an idiot, too, if that helps?' says Harry. 'We all do.'

Miles pulls a face. 'It doesn't help, but thanks for pointing it out.'

'Err, guys,' says Luke, stopping in his tracks, 'why are Falford Town wearing their usual kit?'

We look over, following his gaze. Sure enough, at the other end of the pitch, the opposition team are warming up in their normal strip.

'Didn't make much of an effort to look like Santas, did they?' says Brandon, annoyed.

'But if they're not dressed up, don't they lose?' asks Dave, confused.

'Maybe they didn't read the rules,' suggests Luke.

A few of them have seen us. They laugh and point, until the entire team are looking in our direction. They think it's hilarious that we look like characters from a pantomime.

I feel my confidence disappear. 'We can't play them looking like this.'

'We have to,' says Dave. 'We don't have time to get changed.'

At that moment, a voice calls from behind. 'Something the matter, lads?'

I swivel around to find myself face-to-face with Tristan and his buddies. They're in their designer tracksuits and a couple of them have their phones out, taking pictures of us in our ridiculous outfits.

'What are you doing here?' I ask. 'You lost the tournament, remember?'

'We're just here to watch the final,' he says. 'Couldn't miss out on this, could we, boys?'

His mates smirk and shake their heads.

'Those elf costumes really suit you,' says Bryant.

'He's even the right size for an elf,' says Tristan, pointing to me.

That makes my blood boil. 'We had to wear these. It's in the rules. We had a letter from the council.'

Tristan raises his eyebrows. 'Shame the other team didn't get a letter like that, isn't it? It's almost like someone might have sent it as a joke.'

It takes a few moments for what he's said to sink in. Then, I realise what he's done. Tristan's dad works for the council. There must be paper with the council logo on it all over his house. 'You sent the letter?'

'I don't know what you're on about, Sullivan.' That's what he says. But he also gives me a sly smile. He did it, alright. It's the perfect prank. Even Sergeant Brillin didn't realise we were being led on.

And now, we've shown up to the Christmas Cup final looking like idiots.

'I told you we shouldn't wear them,' mutters Kris.

No-one replies. We're all too shocked by the realisation that Tristan has humiliated us, and there's nothing we can do.

Tristan steps right up to me, his face inches from mine. 'I told you I'd get my revenge, Sullivan. I may have had to kiss your boots, but I'd rather do that than play a match wearing tights and an elf hat. I hope it doesn't ruin your chances of winning the Christmas Cup.'

'It won't,' says Brandon, pulling me away. 'These tights are pretty comfortable. And I'd rather be wearing these clothes than be stuck with your face. Right, lads?'

'Right,' we agree.

It's a good comeback, even if it isn't true. Tristan is as good-looking as Theo, and he knows it.

We walk away from our tormentors.

'I can't believe he did that,' says Luke. 'We should have been suspicious the moment we got that letter.'

'Why would we?' I say. 'Even your dad thought it was legit.'

'But, guys, we can't go ahead with the match now,' says Kris. 'We look stupid.'

'Oh, we're playing alright,' says Brandon. 'Most people have seen us already, so what do we have to lose? The best thing we can do now is win this thing.'

'Brandon's right,' I say. 'We're not going home with our tails between our legs, just because of Tristan's prank. If anyone asks, we say we wanted to do this for a bit of fun.'

'Are we agreed?' asks Dave, looking round.

The others nod. 'Agreed.'

Tristan's had his fun.

Now, it's time for ours.

18. FINAL

We play better than ever.

I'm not sure if it's because we feel like we have something to prove, or whether the elf costumes help us enjoy the game more than we otherwise would. But, either way, we dominate the field from kick-off.

Falford Town are a decent team, but it must be hard to play against a bunch of elves. The costumes seem to distract them. They're not sure whether to take us seriously. That's a mistake.

Brandon might look like he comes from the North Pole, but he moves much faster than any elf should. He'd give Santa's reindeer a run for their money.

Meanwhile, Rex seems to have twice as much magic. The ball moves around him like it's on a string, every touch and flick confusing the Falford defence.

Dave and Theo dance around in midfield like they're at a Christmas party. I've never seen them move with so much energy. They scoop up every loose ball, intercept every Falford pass.

And on the odd occasions the ball gets through to our

defence, a red and white striped foot blocks every shot.

Once we're playing, I can't help but smile at the silliness of it. Even though we should be embarrassed, we're enjoying ourselves.

Somehow, the costumes stop us taking ourselves so seriously. But, that doesn't make our game worse. It makes us better.

Who knew?

We take an early lead, and the crowd whoop and cheer. They're rooting for us. That boosts my confidence. People like the fact we've dressed up. It's helping them to get into the Christmas spirit. They want the elves to win! And the little kids can't take their eyes of us. We just made their Christmas.

After a while, I don't even think about what we're wearing. Ok, so I'm the kid who's been on a national advert for a bedwetting blanket, and now I'm playing football in front of hundreds of people dressed like an elf.

My reputation can't get any worse.

I figure there's no point worrying about that.

Right now, I just have to focus on the game.

At half-time, we're leading two goals to nil. By full-time, Falford have all but given up and we win 4-0.

The only thing worse than being dressed like elves is being battered by a team of them. As soon as the ref blows the whistle, the Falford players shuffle off the field, disappointed.

I've been so focused on the game that I haven't thought about what's at stake. Not until Luke and Dave pull me into a hug, bringing me back to my senses.

It's then that I realise.

This was the final.

We've won the Christmas Cup!

***

The photographer can't believe his luck when we line up to get the trophy. He's got the perfect picture for the local paper.

The other person who can't believe his luck is Sergeant Brillin. He beams at us all. 'You played like champions out there, lads.'

Luke grins back at him. 'Yeah, well you know us elves. We like to work our magic.'

'Maybe we should wear this every time we play?' says Brandon.

Several people punch him for that comment, me included.

'What inspired you to dress like that?' asks Councillor Wellard, as he shakes Sergeant Brillin's hand.

The sergeant frowns and pulls the crumpled letter out of his pocket. 'We got this letter from you.'

The councillor scans the letter, confused. 'I didn't send this.'

I decide to explain. 'Your son did. He thought it'd be funny if we all showed up in these costumes.'

'Is that true?' Councillor Wellard scans the crowd for Tristan, who's trying to slip away. 'Tristan! Get here now!'

His son skulks over, looking mutinous.

'Are you responsible for this letter?'

'No, Dad. I have no idea what they're on about.'

'Don't lie to me, son. Someone wrote it, and it wasn't me.' Barry Wellard isn't a nice man. We've had run-ins with him before. He looks furious that Tristan has stolen some of his council stationery for his schoolboy prank.

'Fine. I did it,' admits Tristan. 'But it was just a joke.'

His dad turns back to Sergeant Brillin. 'I'm sorry my son did that, Sergeant. Trust me, he will regret it. I think he just volunteered to do all the washing up after Christmas dinner.'

Tristan groans. I wouldn't want to be in his shoes when they get home.

'We didn't mind dressing up, did we boys?' says Sergeant Brillin. It's easy for him to say, as he didn't have to do it. I'm not sure he'd be so laid back if he was wearing striped tights.

But, truthfully, it hasn't been as bad as I expected. 'I think it made us play better,' I admit. 'In a way, Tristan did us a massive favour.'

That's another kick in the gut for the bully. He wanted to make us lose, not win. He scowls.

'It gained us a lot of support from the crowd,' says Miles. 'They loved us out there.'

'Well, you'll get a brand new strip in the new year. I'll send the sergeant the details.'

'Smile for the camera, boys,' says the photographer, who's still buzzing around like an annoying wasp. Just how many pictures does he want?

But, I don't mind.

It's nice to have another excuse to hold up the trophy and cheer.

***

We're still on the field when Sergeant Brillin brings out two bags full of presents. It's time for the Secret Santa.

A few of the lads get given theirs. Kris gets some new grip socks. Harry gets a glow-in-the-dark football.

'This one's for you, Jed,' says the sergeant, reaching into the bag.

I've been so caught up with what to buy everyone else, I haven't stopped to think about what I might get. I rip open the small present to discover a pair of soft black gloves, the kind that players wear in the Premiership.

I pull them on, glad to finally have something to protect my hands from the cold. 'They're amazing. Thanks so much to whoever got them!'

A few more presents are handed out, one of them to Brandon. I wonder if he'll like his new kit, or whether I should have just bought myself the Man City shirt instead.

As soon as he opens it, his face lights up. 'Pink and yellow. That's epic! Whoever bought me this is a total legend.'

I can't help grinning. 'I think it'll suit you.'

'Did you get me this? Jed, I love it.'

I act casual. 'Sorry I couldn't get any socks to match.'

'I'll find some.' He grabs hold of me and pulls me into a spontaneous hug. 'Thank you.'

Brandon might be an idiot at times, but I realise right then just how much I love him. Even though he has a wardrobe full of kits, and more money than I could dream of, he's still grateful for the shirt.

I have to admit it was worth sacrificing the top I wanted for this moment.

***

Christmas Day is epic.

Last year, me and Mum spent the day on our own, trying to make the most of it. But it's hard to have that much fun when there's only two of you.

At Dave's, there are loads of people. As well as his immediate family, the grandparents have come along, and there's more food than I've ever seen.

We even take our presents, so we can open them when we're all together.

'Here's yours.' Mum hands me a small, soft parcel. It feels like clothes. I hope it's not underwear, because everyone is watching as I tear off the paper.

A flash of light blue makes my heart skip a beat.

It can't be.

But, it is.

The Man City shirt.

'I'm afraid it's second hand,' she admits, a little embarrassed. 'I got it from the charity shop.'

'Mum, it's amazing.' Even though Dave's family are sitting around, I pull off my t-shirt right there, and tug it on. Then, I give her a massive hug. I'd given up all hope of ever owning this. I can't believe I got the shirt after all. 'I bought you something, too.'

'Jed, you shouldn't have,' she says, as I hand her the tiny gift. Her eyes fill with tears when she unwraps it and opens the box to find the necklace. 'Jed, it's beautiful.'

'I wanted to get you something special,' I say, a lump in my throat.

'It's perfect. Help me put it on.'

I hang the chain around her neck and fasten it at the back.

I can tell she loves it. All afternoon, she fiddles with the pendant, and I catch her checking herself in the mirror.

It's the first time I've got her a proper gift with my own money, and it's the best thing I've ever done.

I might have had to be publicly humiliated on social media to get it, but you know what? I'd do it all again, if I had to, just for this moment.

I realise that Rev Mandy was right.

It really is better to give than to receive, and I get to do both.

And, I figure something else. Perhaps Brandon isn't the luckiest kid alive, after all.

Maybe, it's me.

A NOTE FROM THE AUTHOR

Thanks for reading 'The Christmas Cup'.

I hope you enjoyed it, and you're looking forward to hearing more stories about Jed and the Ferndale Foxes. If you haven't read them yet, then make sure you get hold of the other books in the series. And it would be a huge help to me if you would get your parents to post a review on Amazon for this book. Could you do that? I promise I read every review!

You can connect with my readers' club at:

www.subscribepage.io/footballkids

If you're under thirteen, your parents will need to sign up for you. I'll keep you informed of any new releases, as well as giving you opportunities to get freebies, prizes and giveaways.

Also, check out my Instagram **@zacmarksauthor** where I post football forfeit challenges, where kids sometimes end up egged or with boots full of shaving foam! Check it out and get your parents to message me if you want a challenge of your own!

Finally, can I encourage you to donate some clothes to a local charity shop? It's a great way to recycle stuff, raises money for charity and gives people a cheaper way to buy good quality clothes. It's a win-win!

Stay connected – I love hearing from my readers. Maybe you or your team could make it into one of Jed's adventures!

Thanks so much for being a part of my story.

Zac.

THE CRAFTY COACH

The Ferndale Foxes are in trouble. With no coach, the team will fold.

Jed needs to act fast! He can't imagine life without football. But saving the team is going to be tough: he has to find a way to turn things around, both on and off the pitch.

There's one person who might be able to coach them, but he isn't the kind of person you'd usually ask. Will he be a great choice or will it end in disaster?

THE SNEAKY SUB

It's no fun being on the bench. Jed's finding out the hard way.

Someone isn't playing fair. Jed and his mates are competing for places on the team, but one of his teammates will do anything to keep him off the pitch.

The problem is, he doesn't know who.

He has to solve the mystery, and fast! They're making his life a total misery and they'll stop at nothing to get a game.

But how is he going to find out who's responsible? And what action should he take when he does?

THE GROUNDED GOALIE

Every team needs a goalie. But what if he doesn't show?

Miles is missing and no-one knows why. Jed and his friends need to figure out what's going on. Will Miles ever be allowed to play again?

If not, who's going to take his place? The Ferndale Foxes need to work as a team if they're going to solve the mystery.

But Jed is feeling the pressure. Will he ever get answers, or spend the whole season sliding through mud? And will he be able to save anything, let alone Miles?

THE TERRIBLE TOURNAMENT

It should be the best summer ever. But it's the worst!

When the Ferndale Foxes head off for a football tournament by the sea, they have no idea how tough it will be.

Jed and his teammates can't catch a break, and everything seems to go wrong. Faced with one problem after another, the team falls apart.

It's not easy to stay friends when you feel like a loser.

Will they be able to turn it around before it's too late?

THE PERILOUS PITCH

It's the worst pitch ever. But it's better than nothing.

Now, the council want to take it away.

When Jed and his friends hear there are plans to build on their pitch, they do everything they can to stop it from happening. It's their home ground, and there aren't any other places to play in the village.

But who's going to listen to a group of kids? And how can they make the council change their mind?

DO YOU LOVE FOOTBALL?

Aged 9-13?

Do you eat, sleep and breathe football?

Would you like to take on a challenge?

Want to win some new kit or free books?

Or even appear in one of the books?

Visit **www.subscribepage.io/footballkids** for information on all this and more!